# BLACK RAGE

# BLACK RAGE

BY

*William H. Grier,* M.D.

AND

*Price M. Cobbs,* M.D.

*Foreword by former United States Senator Fred R. Harris*

**BasicBooks**
*A Division of HarperCollins Publishers*

To our intrepid black brothers:

**KEEP ON KEEPING ON!**

# Contents

# Introduction

## *to the 1992 Edition*

While our country struggles to crush recurrent crops of racist behavior, an inspection of our action as a group shows resentment of African Americans to be an integral part of the nation's character. Observers say that democracy is a messy business, with consensus rarely achieved, but for most of U.S. history the majority of white Americans (at least those who determine policy) have been unified on one issue, that of white supremacy.

Save for a few months during the 1960s, it has been the task of African Americans and a few extraordinary whites to set about improving the status of blacks without troubling white America. If blacks are hired into jobs from which they were previously barred, then no white person can be made to feel displaced. Black entrepreneurs are urged to step out onto a "level playing field" where history shows that their creative product, be it land or invention, has been ripped off with no recourse—none whatsoever.

It was with these circumstances facing our country that we wrote *Black Rage* in 1968.

Now new voices rise, saying apparently that African Americans ought to ignore what has happened to them in the past and behave as if we and indeed all Americans were born yesterday.

If the past experience of racism is to be ignored and given no causal weight in explaining the status of blacks in America, then one can only conclude that blacks are poor and disconnected from much of America because of characterological and intellectual deficiencies. With sinister gravity a number of Americans are taking this position.

It ought not to require unusual insight to understand that if a majority tries to dehumanize a minority in order to deny them the benefits of citizenship, it will take a major effort sustained over time to bring all members together again as a comfortable family, a national family. And it surely should require no great sophistication to recognize that the put-upon group will return the resentment of the majority severalfold.

When leaders speak of the irrelevance of race in modern times while the sound of urban gunfire is figuratively heard in the background, how can they or anyone deny, explanatory prefaces aside, that blacks are being attacked because they are black?

Twenty-five years ago, reviewing data during the research and writing of *Black Rage,* we were impressed with the difficulty facing all of us as we travel from child to adult hoping to end up with a reasonably healthy identity and some feeling of self-worth. We marveled then and marvel still at so many African Americans who make this maturational giant step with such success and such grace. America owes black parents an enormous debt for having looked past the negatives, seen the positives, and nourished generations of idealistic Americans.

With this new edition of *Black Rage,* we welcome the continued interest in the issues of race, child development, and society, and of oppression and its consequences for the oppressor and the oppressed.

There are currently serious discussions nationwide on the importance of race, gender, culture, and the problems that attend a diverse people trying to live together in peace. Among other things the discourse asks whether ours is to be a "color-blind" melting pot or a pluralistic puree with all major differences rubbed away. We want to remind readers that the American identity is rooted in a historical event—slavery—and serious work must be done to bring us all farther from that agony.

Attitudes toward blacks that have their origin in slavery shape the nation's response to citizens of all colors, and the same attitudes have an enormous impact on the conduct of foreign policy.

We choose to be optimistic about the future of America, but it is perilous to deny the past. If this book can be a reminder of where we have been, the authors will be satisfied.

# Introduction

## *to the Paperback Edition*

In 1966, when this book was first conceived, we aimed to write a clinical handbook spelling out in the clearest possible language certain special aspects of the psychiatric treatment of blacks— things we had learned in our own years of clinical experience and in the steady challenge to bring the best of a limited body of clinical skills to the aid of people with immediate problems. We were dismayed that so little writing of this kind was available to the therapists being trained in increasing numbers and in a variety of disciplines. We felt that the technical language of psychiatry was so ripe for misunderstanding that we wanted wherever possible to avoid its jargon. We chose the clearest possible English and addressed it to those thousands upon thousands of therapists, black and white, for whom such clinical material was otherwise not available. Fortunately our work found the audience we wanted, and a larger one besides.

We were, of course, gratified when *Black Rage* found such a large audience when it was originally published. For a reissue, however, a word of caution is in order. A new generation of readers must first acquaint or reacquaint itself with the sweeping and traumatic events that occurred in the decade before the book was written. During that time, there occurred in our nation extremes of intense social ferment and national self-scrutiny, as smoldering racial tensions ar        torical grievances suddenly— or so it was thought—erupted, and demands were made for immediate and lasting change.

The cutting edge of black protest focused first on legal discrimination in the South, then on racial prejudice exhibited nationwide by whites, and finally on the racism historically imbedded in the institutions and people of this most democratic of nations. These explosive issues came close to tearing the nation apart, and many Americans were jolted in a most deeply personal way.

As a consequence, many individuals, patient and therapist

# INTRODUCTION

alike, searched for the essence of what it means to be a black American in a nation that reserved (and in many instances continues to reserve) a uniquely disfavored place for its black citizens. This search compelled many people to re-examine that always delicate balance between the ills of individuals and the ills of their society. The question was asked silently and stridently: What part of my problems, discomforts, and deprivations is caused my own inadequacies and what part by my place in a society?

For many blacks the search required a more refined understanding of their society before they could more completely understand themselves. And ultimately most black Americans came to realize that only by understanding both themselves and their society can either be changed. Focusing on that delicate balance and bringing clinical insights and clarity to it was one of the primary challenges in writing *Black Rage*.

That, however, was in 1966; and now some fourteen years later there is an abundance of material written by thoughtful, knowledgeable clinicians rich in experience, and touching on areas of the problem we knew not of in 1966. It is exciting to witness the scholarship now focused on the mental health of blacks, the factors affecting it, and the remedies as well. In the face of such impressive work we would have been reluctant to present a reissue of *Black Rage* save for one reason: the more we learn about the complexities of black and white life in America, the more we see there is to learn.

Our federal government, for example, owes much of its structure and function to the continuing efforts of the white majority to formalize fluctuating attitudes toward black Americans.

The American economy and its political expressions bear evidence of the struggle of a people who think of themselves as basically generous and democratic—to seize the main chance, to win at all costs, to minimize competition, and, in fact, to tolerate no competition at all from black citizens. White citizens at times exhibit the skills of ideological contortionists.

Clinicians are dissuaded from such critical thoughts, however, by the demands of patients, and the present situation is but a backdrop against which troubled people seek to work out the unique wonders of their own lives.

Our original goal remains unchanged—a clinical handbook

illustrating certain unique aspects of psychotherapy with blacks, with the added note that now many more authors have much to share on the subject.

The gravest danger we see is that unscrupulous people may use psychotherapy with blacks as a means of social control, to persuade the patient to be satisfied with his lot. Such would be a wicked abuse of the confidence of the unwitting patient as well as of the confidence invested in professionals by the community. There will no doubt always be wicked persons capable of such things.

The most important aspect of therapy with blacks, we are convinced, is that racist mistreatment must be echoed and underlined as a fact, an unfortunate fact, but a most important fact—a part of reality. Dissatisfaction with such mistreatment is to be expected, and one's resentment should be of appropriate dimensions. It bears some resemblance to military psychiatry, where the psychiatrist must keep fit for duty the warrior whose primary function is to oppose the enemy. In America the role of blacks, as for humans everywhere, is to live and flourish and to be fit progenitors of generations to come. To do so, they must oppose racism in an unrelenting way. Psychiatry for such warriors aims to keep them fit for the duty at hand and healthy enough to enjoy the victories that are certain to come.

# Foreword

*by United States Senator Fred R. Harris*

When my colleagues and I on the National Advisory Commission on Civil Disorders concluded that the deepest cause of the recent riots in our cities was white racism, we went as directly as we knew how to the heart of the matter.

To be sure, there are many evils which derive from racism that are more easily identified, including the existence of ghetto neighborhoods, joblessness, stultifying classrooms, and poor health. But there should be no mistake about this, for the future of America is too important: the root cause of the black wrath that now threatens to destroy this nation is the unwillingness of white Americans to accept Negroes as fellow human beings. This is precisely what we meant by racism.

This book is crucially important because it, too, goes to the heart of the matter. I can only hope its message is heeded. That message is simple—that despite the passage of five civil rights bills since 1957, despite the erosion of legal supports for segregated institutions, despite greater acceptance of Negroes into our major institutions, both public and private, it is still no easy thing to be a black person in America. As the authors put it, this is to say that for the average Negro "so much time has passed and so little has changed."

What does this mean? The answer is clear, yet terribly difficult for most of us to see—that "the civilization that tolerated slavery dropped its slaveholding cloak but the inner feelings remained . . . [that] the practice of slavery stopped over a hundred years ago, *but the minds of our citizens have never been freed.*"

The authors as psychiatrists are admirably equipped to see that white perceptions of Negroes, and the historical inculcation of these perceptions in the minds of Negroes themselves, are at the root of our present troubles. They demonstrate beyond challenge the crippling effects of white American culture on the attempts of Negro Americans to do here what all people everywhere must do if they are to develop fully—to find an identity, a sense of worth, to relate to others, to love, to work, and to create. Black rage is the result of our failure, after 300 years, to make these human values possible.

Many of the cases that the authors discuss will no doubt fascinate you as they fascinate me. They are in most cases ordinary people doing or attempting to do ordinary things, but handicapped by one thing above all else—that they are black people in a white man's culture. These cases, the authors argue, reveal much, as earlier discussions of mental disorders always have, about the society in which they occur. That the message is unpleasant goes without saying. It reveals in a thousand subtle ways the shortcomings of this land in its struggle to realize its central values —individual freedom and equality.

Without question the hour is late and the message of this book is grim. But the restoration of domestic tranquility to this land depends on our understanding and heeding it.

*Washington, D.C.*
*May 1968*

# BLACK RAGE

# I

# *Who's Angry?*

What the hell do niggers want anyway?

Every other ethnic group has made it up the ladder on its own. Why don't the blacks do likewise?

They keep raving about their rights. Well, white people have rights too.

These and similar comments have been the voice of white America lashing back at the growing unrest of Negroes. Black people continue to revolt against laws and customs that are deadly and humiliating. The voice of black America has been heard in the explosions of Watts, Newark, and Detroit.

Aggression leaps from wounds inflicted and ambitions spiked. It grows out of oppression and capricious cruelty.

It is logical and predictable if we know the soil from which it comes.

People bear all they can and, if required, bear even more. But if they are black in present-day America they have been asked to shoulder too much. They have had all they can stand. They will be harried no more. Turning from their tormentors, they are filled with rage.

The growing anger of Negroes is frightening to white America. There is a feeling of betrayal and undeserved attack. White people have responded with a rage of their own. As the lines become more firmly drawn, exchange of information is the first casualty.

If racist hostility is to subside, and if we are to avoid open conflict on a nationwide scale, information is the most desperately needed commodity of our time.

And of the things that need knowing, none is more important than that all blacks are angry. White Americans seem not to recognize it. They seem to think that all the trouble is caused by only a few "extremists." They ought to know better. We have talked to many Negroes under the most intimate of circumstances and we know better.

By way of introduction we would have the reader meet three black people who are not in open rebellion against anyone. They are simply trying to live out their lives in as fulfilling a way as circumstances will allow.

They are typical of black Americans, held tight in a snare, coming more and more to realize that even their inner suffering is due largely to a hostile white majority and, with this realization, gaining a determination to change that hostile society.

## Roy

Roy was a painter. On the job, he worked on the highest scaffolds that were flung up around buildings. He worked desperately hard, saved his money, and looked forward to a career as a professional golfer. In a trade in which speed and skill paid off, he was a good painter and made a handsome living.

One Friday afternoon he slipped and fell thirty feet to the ground. He landed in soft sand inches from a stake which might have impaled him. He was afraid that his injuries might be permanent, but aside from a few aches he was found well enough by the doctor at the dispensary. He was sent home and was told to check later with his family doctor.

Driving home, he felt a sharp pain in his groin which lasted through the night. The next day a back pain sent him to the hospital. Prior to the accident he had been in excellent health and a rapid recovery was expected. His body was a well-functioning machine. He exercised regularly and maintained robust health. He looked forward to the time when he could give up hard labor and devote full time to the more glamorous life of a golf professional.

When discharged from the hospital he was told that everything was functioning as it should and that he could return to work. And he would have, except for his worry about a symptom to which little attention had been paid. Outside the hospital the problem became all-consuming: he was unable to have an erection.

His physicians found no organic basis for the com-

5

plaint. There had been no nerve damage to his spine and no injury to his genital organs. After repeated tests which offered no explanation, they recommended that he see a psychiatrist.

He was skeptical of this advice and recited the story of his fall to the psychiatrist. He told of having been the third of six children born in the rural South. His father was a gambler and small-time con artist who did not support the family and only visited them from time to time. Roy remembered him as a cruel man who beat him viciously on the occasion of each visit.

His mother was a hard-working, resourceful woman who supported her children by doing domestic work for white families. She too was cruel. She beat the children regularly and Roy recalls how difficult it was to be friendly with her. In a moment of tenderness she would sometimes strike him, remembering some misdemeanor which had escaped punishment. Life was squalid and humiliating and Roy left soon after graduating from high school.

He was ambitious. He exercised with weights and played golf daily, having learned the game in the South as a caddy. As we noted earlier, he worked long hours and saved his money. He always volunteered for the most hazardous jobs and on most jobs worked near the top of the building.

He felt that the only way to get out of the ghetto was to work hard. He exhausted himself on the job. He went to Alaska, where the pay was higher, giving no thought to the greater danger in the more hazardous work there. He was black and he felt that superhuman efforts were required to "make it." He was a driven man.

*Who's Angry?*

He had been married for about a year before he fell, and his sexual life, like his work, was vigorous. He had intercourse two, three, and four times nightly. His wife, whose previous husband had failed to satisfy her sexually, was delighted with his performance and felt that their marriage was largely founded on his prodigious capacities.

For years Roy had carried within him the fear that he would not "make it" and would have to return to the small town of his birth as a failure. After the accident he had dreams of falling from a building and shattering on impact as though made of glass.

He had seen himself as a lone wolf, working hard, facing barriers, overcoming them, and moving up. Hard work would pay off. In this attitude he recognized some characteristics of his mother and stated flatly that he had no wish to be like his father.

With the fall his world crumbled. He could not work; he became afraid of heights. He nagged his wife for reassurance, and made so much of his impotence that she left him. He was anxious, unable to sleep, and he was reduced finally to receiving public assistance. He brooded over his impotence and considered suicide.

His unraveling after the accident emphasized the fragility of his previous functioning. One might speculate at great length about his castration anxiety and counterphobic functioning at work. But he was concerned about failing even before the fall. He seemed primed for a dissolution of his comfortable world and a return to the South. He seemed to feel that he had no right to do well. He said finally that, coming as he did from the squalor of the black ghetto, he had done well to stay up as long as he had. He expected to end up crushed, down and out. It was as if the proper place in life for him was as an ineffectual, defenseless, castrated man, and that his brief period of competence was but a temporary violation of the natural order of things.

Roy's illness revolved in large measure around his conception of his place in the world. The subtle dynamics that led to his fall and subsequent symptomatology were encompassed within a larger social dynamic which was in motion before his birth. For three hundred years his "place" in America had been shaped by powerful forces, and the small drama of his own life becomes magnified in the shaping of a nation and multiplied by his twenty million brethren.

## Bertha

Bertha was born in the South, the "baby daughter" of an unusual Negro farm family. They were landowners and her father was a man of pride and courage who had survived. She recalled an example of his strength from her childhood. A white man once spoke insultingly to her mother and sister. Her father, an older man, beat the white man senseless. By some means or other he managed to avoid the reprisals, legal and otherwise, of the white community.

Bertha was a dark girl with thick lips and a flat nose. When she was sent to a nearby city to school, she lived with relatives who considered her homely and unsophisticated. She was a spirited child, however, and reminded them that she was receiving excellent grades while her "attractive" city cousins were barely passing. She was in fact very bright and graduated from a mediocre college with high marks.

As a young woman she moved from the South to a large city and sought employment as a schoolteacher. She was told that the college she had attended was too poor academically for her to qualify and it would be necessary for her to take additional courses. This she did, working in a menial job part time and going to school.

She was busy climbing over an unnecessary series of hurdles and it was significant that she selected this time to enter upon a miserable marriage. The man she chose was an uneducated laborer, who was bitter and envious of her education. He was physically abusive and degrading in his sexual approach. After one week of marriage she realized it was a mistake.

She later spent considerable time pondering why she had made this marriage, but found it difficult to recall her frame of mind at the time. She could not remember any thought of her childhood which might offer a clue. She had always envisioned herself as a professional woman married to a professional man. Her view of her life had continued in this vein practically up to the time of the marriage. She and her husband remained together a few months, and after the divorce it was as if she had emerged from a bad dream. She continued her studies, finally completing the course and obtaining certification.

She started teaching and soon began a brief affair with a janitor. She described it as a torrid romance which burned itself out in a few months. Again, her partner was an unlettered man, crude and insensitive as a lover.

When she presented herself for treatment she was depressed. She had by this time married a fellow professional and had a small child. Her husband was devoted to her and she to him. They were comfortable financially and her depression was a puzzle to her. "What have I got to be sad about?" There had been the usual illnesses, deaths, and disappointments but none would explain the lingering, brooding quality of her melancholy, which had been with her since shortly after the marriage.

The most careful analysis revealed nothing so remarkable in her early life which might account for her two earlier love relationships and her depression in this marriage. On the surface she seemed to suffer some degradation of love feelings, a distortion which made it possible for her to find pleasure with coarse men whom she felt to be socially beneath her. Similarly, she found little pleasure in the marriage to a "suitable" mate. It is clear that it was necessary for her to suffer in a particular way to experience sexual pleasure. The humiliation she received from her earlier lovers was essential to gratification. The honored role she occupied in her current marriage made it necessary for her to bring about her own suffering in the form of brooding depression.

The dynamics underlying her depression are not unique, but they have a unique quality which is of interest. In her associations she saw herself as a black, ugly, ignorant, dirty little girl who could be loved by no one. She fairly wallowed in the perception of herself as such a creature with degraded sexual appetites. She fantasied herself as a prostitute, a call girl, a promiscuous woman, and the most painful percept was as a helpless sexual object available to contemptuous white men at their whim. To indulge in the latter fantasy was like probing a painful wound.

Her route to the office took her through a section of the city where she saw black prostitutes soliciting white men as they drove past. On occasion she herself would be hailed by one of the white motorists. These events, together with her experiences in the South, served as the nodal point where reality and fantasy fused. She had developed feelings based in part on reality and in part on the most humiliating experience she could imagine.

The point we wish to make is that the most humiliating thing she could conceive lay so close to real experience that it takes a fine eye to separate them. Moreover, the fantasied experience would not have to be manufactured to become real. She had offers from time to time. Ever since her adolescent years the society in which she lived provided an inviting pathway to a degrading way of life.

Her white counterpart may have identical fantasies but the social order has been designed to protect her from her impulses and stands between her and those who would invite her along such a path. In order to live out her fantasies the white girl would have to breach significant social barriers.

Bertha had no such protective barriers and had to struggle alone to avoid such a life. Her depression and its accompanying fantasies, then, had a much deeper quality. She could say: "I know I am a whore at heart— society confirms it." "I know I am suitable only for casual sexual use—society confirms it."

Therefore the task of showing her the neurotic elements in her depression was infinitely greater. She could always turn, not to her infantile conflicts, but to the out-side world, and find confirmation of the distorted view she held of herself. She could justify her interest in the lower-class lovers by this self-percept—they were the appropriate men to share her degraded appetites. Her present husband did not know what a monster he had married. He deserved a good, clean, pretty, light-skinned girl who had more conventional romantic tastes. This idea was supported by the fact that indeed most of his colleagues had married light-skinned Negro women.

As a result of the insidious linking of social oppression and neurotic guilt, Bertha was burdened with a depression which was most refractory to treatment. Long periods were necessary for the careful examination of black-white relations. The influence of history on contemporary life was studied with her. Prostitution and its subtleties, as well as sexuality in general, were examined in great detail with the purpose of objectifying events and social realities and showing that they had an existence *outside herself*. It was necessary to consider in detail what her life might be like in another country which did not have the racist history of the United States.

All this was necessary because she perceived the racial situation in the United States as an intensely *personal* phenomenon. She thought it a fundamental truth that black women with thick lips and short kinky hair were *ugly*. Intellectually she could discuss varying standards of beauty, but they had no relevance for her—*she* was ugly. She felt in her bones that Negroes were helpless in en-counters with white people and that black women were helpless before white men. All these attitudes were not conscious but they were not buried very deep.

It was necessary to help her see that these factors were independent of her. She had to see that beauty depends on the culture and that sexual desire is largely physiology. Only by separating the internal and external factors could she begin to see the neurotic use to which she had put racial prejudice. She could then turn finally to her own troubled development for answers to her current psychological dilemma.

The essence of the situation is that black women have a nearly bottomless well of self-depreciation into which they can drop when depressed. The well is prepared by society and stands waiting, a prefabricated pit which they have had no hand in fashioning.

## John

Let us finally tell you about John. Some years ago he sought psychiatric help because he was facing court action. In an outburst of temper he had injured a fellow worker and was being sued. His lawyer asked for a psychiatrist's statement and wanted it on record that John needed treatment. Initially John made certain that he told only enough to aid in his defense. Soon, however, he dropped his guard and told of his worries about his work record. He was highly trained, had several university degrees, and was currently employed as a professional. The assault jeopardized his job. But, he said, he had regularly found new jobs. He had done well in them and as he rose to the top became increasingly anxious and managed to "louse up the situation." In the end he generally quit the job to find something more promising. Now, however, he was frightened. With a record of assault on the job he might have great difficulty in moving to something better.

In this troubled state he decided to remain in treatment and in the ensuing months the following story emerged.

He was the older of two children. His father had been a sickly man, stern and quick to punish. At times he beat his wife, but withal there was a mood of rectitude, propriety, and great ambition for his son. The older man was never able to work regularly and he died when John was in his late teens.

John's mother worked to supplement the father's pension benefits. She was the strong spine, all-supporting, and unrelenting in prodding the boy to excel in school. She was close to him, his only confidante. He recalled the numerous small ways he tried to break away from her— but always to fall back, to come back to her for solace and understanding. Indeed, he said many times: "She was the only one I could talk to."

His sister seemed unimportant to him. Though bright, she did poorly in school. She became pregnant as an adolescent, married, and now has eight children. Her life is a struggle to support the children. John was ashamed of her. He was brilliant and articulate and had a commanding presence. In school and university his record was outstanding. On new jobs, the initial impression he made was favorable. But he was aware that as time went on he began to gloss over tasks which he chose not to perform. He had a remarkable store of energy and with each new job he began with a flurry of activity. In time, however, he characteristically passed over details, a practice which eventually put him at a disadvantage. In retrospect he pondered why he made these choices which inevitably led to his downfall. On occasion he worked at two full-time jobs and took a full course at the university. His capacity for work seemed unlimited but his capacity for tolerating success was another matter.

He was a passive boy, frightened of his father if he were disobedient and clinging to his mother as her model son.

His crippling symptom, however, had to do with work and, in a larger sense, with success. It all came to focus on a job he obtained while in treatment. He joined an executive training program with a group of eager young men who were to compete against one another for a few positions that led rapidly up the management ladder.

He entered the scene full of confidence and as he compared himself with the others he saw that he had many advantages. He performed brilliantly in the classroom. On occasion he felt dismay over what seemed to be a pervasive confidence in his white middle-class competitors. He observed that he could shake them by displaying greater knowledge but they seemed to possess a resilience which he found difficult to understand since he was convinced that they simply did not know very much.

On the early high tide of success John turned his energies to innovation. Within the first month of training he analyzed the manner in which new material was offered and outlined a method of presentation which was better than the one in use. His superiors were much impressed and incorporated some of his ideas into the training program. They suggested that he might make a significant contribution if he reviewed the complete training program and made suggestions at a later point when he had become more familiar with the total operation of the company.

At about this time the training schedule called for a week of specialized study in another city and John's entire class was flown to that city and given comfortable hotel accommodations. Experts in related fields were brought in to conduct day-long sessions and an intensive intellectual competition among the members of the class was encouraged. John returned from the trip shaken. He said that in the course of the week all his confidence left him. It was hard to judge, but he thought that his general performance was adequate, not outstanding. Of great concern to him were his own inner feelings of incompetence and uncertainty, which were in direct contrast to the feelings he had had prior to attending the conference. The crux of the problem seemed to lie in the luxurious surroundings. John described the plush carpets, the spacious rooms, the thick steaks, and the unlimited supply of liquor, all paid for by the company. And perhaps the most troubling aspect of the whole situation was the ease with which John's white colleagues seemed to accept this bounty as the most natural thing in the world. He described them striding about the rich rooms, smoking cigars, acting as if they were already full-fledged officers of the company. He, on the other hand, felt frightened, out of place, hungry for the money and luxury he saw about him, but fearful that his eagerness and greed might be too apparent and that, having laid eyes on the promised land, it would be snatched away from him. As a result, he felt that he was pressing too hard in the classroom sessions. It was difficult to sleep at night, wondering what might be asked the next day, feeling that upon his answer to each question rested the possibility of being shut out of wealth forever. This experience represented the first downward shift in his functioning and the first serious drop in the high hopes he had brought to the training period.

After his return to the city and the resumption of the ordinary pace of training, his spirits gradually rose and his functioning improved. Neither, however, reached their former heights. The work in therapy now focused on his relationship with others on the job. He was troubled and wanted to establish the "proper" relationship with other Negroes who had jobs inferior to his own. He regarded it as an article of faith that he must do anything and everything to convey to them that he was a "brother." He was ingenious in the clever ways he devised to overcome their initial suspicion of him. He genuinely felt a sense of brotherhood with them and wanted them to know that although he was in an executive training program he had not "abandoned" his own people.

He felt uneasy with white employees at a level below his own. He wanted friendly relationships with them but was afraid that those who had strong anti-Negro feelings would seize every opportunity to sabotage him. He felt he could ill afford to befriend a person who might jeopardize this valuable opportunity. On occasion, the genuine openness and friendliness of a white subordinate overcame John's apprehension and he responded with a flood of friendship. At other times, his suspicion was confirmed by some minor treachery and he pulled back to resume an attitude of circumspection. On one occasion an immediate superior suggested that he take more care with his dress, pointing out that his shoes were not shined and that his suit looked a bit seedy. This hurt him deeply and he resolved never to dress in a way that would expose him to such pain again.

On previous jobs when his superiors were female he was aware that he performed better. He seemed always able to do well under these circumstances and to impress his superiors with a fine performance. In this company all his superiors were men and he never felt that they fully appreciated the high quality of his work and the full range of his potential. In this connection his dreams were particularly helpful. He was apprehensive and troubled about the prospect of success on the job and he had recurrent dreams of returning to the old neighborhood and to the household of his childhood. His associations made it clear that the house and neighborhood expressed a longing for the comforting presence of a mother who had played an important and reassuring role in his early years. Further, his dreams on numerous occasions wove together images of his boss and his father into a frightening composite man who pursued him with deadly intent. The nightmare quality of these dreams reflected his more anguished moments on the job. They also helped him to understand how it was that he was so easily made anxious by a male superior.

While the training program was complex and comprehensive, the essential skill to be mastered and demonstrated was the capacity for supervision. This was the crux of the matter. The company wanted capable, skillful, resourceful supervisors and wanted to weed out under the pressure of competition those aspirants who did not have this capacity. When this became clear John was troubled by the difficulty he had in being firm with subordinates.

With Negro subordinates he thought he would be misunderstood and that they would think him even more white than his colleagues. Not wanting to give such an impression, he was in conflict when called upon to judge his Negro subordinates.

He was in a different kind of quandary with his white subordinates. He was afraid that if he were too firm with them they would complain that he was abusing his position and using his advantage to act out his own anti-white feelings. The problem was further complicated in that some of his subordinates were white women who on occasion were seductive in their behavior. He was particularly alarmed when he found himself attracted to one such woman and went to extraordinary efforts to avoid being in her presence. With others he was tormented with the fear that when he declined their invitations they would retaliate in some manner that would place him in jeopardy.

When, as a result of therapeutic efforts, he was able to be relatively objective and render a firm disciplinary judgment without reference to race or sex, he felt that a milestone had been passed.

As the training continued John had periods of high excitement and alternating moods of depression. He was exhilarated by his triumphs and devastated by his setbacks. Throughout the lengthening period, however, there was a nagging concern over a particular area of his work. From time to time he would dismiss it from his mind, hoping that he would eventually improve in this area, and on other occasions he would struggle with it briefly but the matter seemed never to be set right. As the details of his work came into sharper focus in therapy and in his own mind, it became clear that the area of uncertainty was the one area of his functioning with the company which was of most importance to profits, having to do with sales and collections. At about this time his supervisor called him in and told him that his continuing deficiency was serious and was likely to jeopardize his success in the program. John felt trapped and tried desperately to do better, but to no avail. His depression deepened, his efficiency dropped, and he was finally dismissed as a failure.

This story of an eager aspirant for the rewards of this society who was caught in snares, some but not all of his own making, may appear to be unexceptional and in no way different from the story which might be told of his white colleagues who also failed at the task. The point we wish to make by means of this unhappy chronicle has to do with the setting in which it takes place—the setting, that is, as John sees it. We take the position that his view of his world is central to his ability to succeed. We seek in no way to minimize the importance of his intrapsychic experiences, nor would we minimize the importance of the intrapersonal involvements which played such an important part. We simply mean to say that it is very much like the common dynamics of a man and a woman meeting and falling in love. The relationship might be identical whether the couple be a pair of black migrant farm workers or a well-to-do young white couple in an affluent Connecticut suburb. We simply say that the course of their love will be profoundly influenced by the world in which they live and the manner in which they see their world.

In like manner, the aspirant for an important position may succeed or fail according to his own brilliance, stupidity, avarice, or self-destructive trends. His success or failure may in addition be burdened by the prejudice of white employers. We seek to focus attention on the man's reaction to failure.

John found himself profoundly intimidated by the luxury he encountered during the week-long training period. He felt himself tempted by greed to offer any part of himself, or all of himself, in exchange for such riches. He was alarmed by his reaction and it made him even more afraid that, coming so close, he might now fail to perform and lose this opportunity.

He experienced considerable anxiety when he found it necessary to wield power over others. The therapeutic work with him made it clear that this situation reactivated conflicts regarding identification with his father, but in a larger sense he was troubled by a realistic concern having to do with the uneasy position of a black man wielding power in a hostile white society. To do so brought him into direct competition with white men in a frankly open encounter.

John's milieu from cradle to consultation room had put a penalty on success. He was allowed to be outstanding among black people but was penalized when he competed successfully against whites. This was consistent with his experience as a child. His parents were accepting of his achievements as an obedient child, but they were critical of any advance beyond childhood. The environment of his adult life was then perceived as reinforcing an unfortunate aspect of his family experience. He was encouraged to be an outstanding "child Negro" but harsh penalties were invoked if he behaved as an adult. This powerful interlocking of family milieu and social attitudes has presented a barrier to him and his black brethren which is felt by no other ethnic group in America.

One of the problems in understanding the discontent of black people in America is highlighted in this material. The relationship between intrapsychic functioning and the larger social environment is exceedingly complex. Among other things, Negroes want to change inside but find it difficult to do so unless things outside are changed as well. It is clear that the simplistic solution of "more education" is meaningless when a society is more attuned to race than it is to academic achievement.

Finally, the complex milieu in which American Negroes live has been shaped by their presence and continues to alter its form in response to this troublesome tenth of the population.

# II

# *The Shadow of the Past*

Americans characteristically are unwilling to think about the past. We are a future-oriented nation, and facing backward is an impediment to progress. Although these attitudes may propel us to the moon, they are deficient when human confli    eds resolution. They bring white Americans to an impasse when they claim to "understand" black people. After all, the thoughts begin, the Negro is also an American and if he is different it is only a matter of degree. Clichés are brought forth and there is a lengthy recitation of the names of famous Negroes. Long association has bred feelings of familiarity which masquerade as knowledge. But there remain puzzles about black people; all is not understood; something is missing.

For if the black American is to be truly understood, his history must be made intelligible. It is a history that is interwoven with that of this country, although it is rarely reported with candor. In recent years superficial studies of Negroes have been made. For those few who truly search, the past of the black man is seen reflected in his daily life.

It is evident in character structure and child-rearing. It can be heard on a Sunday morning in a Baptist church. It reveals itself in the temper of the ghetto and in the emerging rage now threatening to shatter this nation, a nation the black man helped to build. A few black people may hide their scars, but most harbor the wounds of yesterday.

The black man of today is at one end of a psychological continuum which reaches back in time to his enslaved ancestors. Observe closely a man on a Harlem street corner and it can be seen how little his life experience differs from that of his forebears. However much the externals differ, their inner life is remarkably the same.

On a cold morning one of the authors sat watching a group of black men. They were standing outside an office for casual laborers in clusters of four or five. Some were talking and gesturing, but from a distance one could detect apathy in most.

These were the "hard-core" unemployed. Their difficulties could be blamed on lack of education, personal maladjustments, or just plain laziness and such a judgment would be partially correct. The greater truth was that they were black. Because of this fact, they had little chance of obtaining favorable or permanent work. They were doomed to spend endless gray mornings hoping to secure a day's work.

A truck drove up and they stiffened. There was a ripple of excitement as a white man leaned out of the cab and squinted. As he ran his eyes past the different men, one could almost hear his thoughts.

*This one is too thin . . . that dark one looks smart-alecky and is probably slow . . . the boy way in the back there might do.*

No imagination is required to see this scene as a direct remnant of slavery. Move back in time and this could be an auction block. The manual labor is the same and so is the ritual of selection. The white man involved in the selection feels he is only securing a crew. But, then, so did his forefathers. In addition, the psychic structure of the black men being selected has altered little since slavery. To know this is deeply troubling—and frightening.

A city erupts in fury. Its residents are appalled and outraged. Biracial committees are appointed and scapegoats appear from everywhere. Instead of wretched housing and stifling unemployment, outside agitators and wily Communists are said + be the most important causes. Always the basic reason. .e at best minimized and at worst denied. After three centuries of oppression the black man is still thought to need a provocateur to inflame him!

History is forgotten. There is little record of the first Africans brought to this country. They were stripped of everything. A calculated cruelty was begun, designed to crush their spirit. After they were settled in the white man's land, the malice continued. When slavery ended and large-scale physical abuse was discontinued, it was supplanted by different but equally damaging abuse. The cruelty continued unabated in thoughts, feelings, intimidation and occasional lynching. Black people were consigned to a place outside the human family and the whip of the plantation was replaced by the boundaries of the ghetto.

The culture of slavery was never undone for either master or slave. The civilization that tolerated slavery dropped its slaveholding cloak but the inner feelings remained. The "peculiar institution" continues to exert its evil influence over the nation. The practice of slavery stopped over a hundred years ago, but the minds of our citizens have never been freed.

To be a bondsman was to experience a psychological development very different from the master's. Slavery required the creation of a particular kind of person, one *compatible* with a life of involuntary servitude. The ideal slave had to be absolutely dependent and have a deep consciousness of personal inferiority. His color was made the badge of that degradation. And as a final precaution, he was instilled with a sense of the unlimited power of his master. Teachings so painstakingly applied do not disappear easily.

The white man tried to justify the lot of the slave in many ways. One explanation made the slave a simple child who needed the protective guardianship of a benevolent parent. For many whites this distortion has persisted to the present. A modern version holds that black people are little different from other citizens save for a paucity of education and money. The reason for these deficiencies is left vague. The observer is left with the comfortable feeling that blacks are stunted in growth, have profligate ways, and are uninterested in learning. This attitude obscures the multitude of wrongs and the ruthless oppression of blacks, from slavery to now.

The Negro man of eighty told a story. He was twelve and a playmate was tied in a cage waiting to be taken away and lynched. The shackled boy stood accused of raping a white woman.

The old man recalled the fright which caused him to run away the next day. From that time on he never knew a home. His years were spent roaming about the country. He became an itinerant preacher, forever invoking God, but always too terrified to return to his place of birth. When asked why, he would reply: "The white folks down there are too mean."

For most of his life he was tortured by memories. Every place he stopped, he soon became frightened and moved on. Sometimes in the middle of a sermon he would cry out:

"How could they do that to a boy?"

This old man is even now living in one of our cities. He continues to preach in storefront churches. At times he may encounter whites 	o smile benevolently at his quaintness and apparent exaggerations. But his memories are real and his hatred, however masked, is a burning fire.

Because of an inattention to history, the present-day Negro is compared unfavorably with other racial and ethnic groups who have come to this country. Major differences in backgrounds are ignored. The black man was brought to this country forcibly and was completely cut off from his past. He was robbed of language and culture. He was forbidden to be an African and never allowed to be an American. After the first generation and with each new group of slaves, the black man had only his American experience to draw on. For most Negroes, the impact of the experience has been so great as to even now account for a lack of knowledge of their past.

This can be contrasted with the heritage of the American Indian. He truly has known the violence of white America, but his legacies are of a different sort. Now, decimated and forlorn, survivors can nevertheless tell tales of past glories. At least in reliving the time when his people ruled the land, the Indian can vicariously achieve a measure of dignity.

Various groups that have come to these shores have been able to maintain some continuity of social institutions. In the process of Americanization, they have retained an identification with their homeland. The Chinese, who in many instances functioned virtually as slaves, were allowed to preserve a family structure. Other oppressed groups, notably the Irish and Italians, were never infused with the shame of color. In addition, they had the protection and support of the Roman Catholic Church. Except for the Negro, all sizable groups in America have been able to keep some old customs and traditions.

The black experience in this country has been of a different kind. It began with slavery and with a rupture of continuity and an annihilation of the past. *Even now each generation grows up alone.* Many individual blacks feel a desperate aloneness not readily explained. The authors have heard stories telling of each generation's isolation from every other. Non-black groups pass on proud traditions, conscious of the benefit they are conferring. For black people, values and rituals are shared and indeed transmitted, but with little acknowledgment of their worth. The Jew achieves a sense of ethnic cohesiveness through religion and a pride in background, while the black man stands in solitude.

There are other comparisons and Negroes participate in them. The white American has created a blindness for himself which has a peculiar effect on blacks. In psychotherapeutic sessions Negroes are preoccupied with determining just how many of their difficulties are a consequence of the prejudice of whites. And while there is sometimes the tendency to attribute everything to white cruelty, there is often the opposite tendency—a determination not to see. They may insist that white oppression has never exerted any influence on their lives, even in the face of such realities as police brutality, job and housing discrimination, and a denial of educational opportunities. It is a powerful national trait, this willful blindness to the abuse of blacks in America. It is a blindness that includes the victim as well as the crime.

An eighty-seven-year-old woman was born in the deep South, the result of a union between one of the black "girls on the place" and the son o    white landowner. Years later she was told how, at her birth, the white mistress of the "big house" heard that her son had fathered a child. The young mother was summoned to bring the child for an audience with the grandmother.

The old lady admired the child, and noting her fairness, suggested that she be taken and raised as white.

The mother objected: "She is my child and I'll keep her."

Even into old age, this Negro woman admired the courage of her mother. She spoke about the thin line separating the races. A flip of the coin could decide whether one was "colored" or "white."

The relationship between black and white is complex. This association has affected the white partner less than the black, but the effect on the white partner has had more significance since he has been the policy maker. An analysis of the relationship tells much about the American national character. Attitudes of the kind directed toward blacks, rooted deep in the fabric of this country, clearly have significant influence on many decisions. A nation which has made the despising of blacks a unique element of its identity is at a profound disadvantage when called upon to lock arms with people of other lands and form a brotherhood of nations.

A focus on the black partner yields information of a different sort. To be "colored" has meant far more than riding in the back of the bus. To be sure, there is great misery in being the last hired and first fired and relegated to decaying sections of town, but there is enduring grief in being made to feel inferior.

The old woman may have been fortunate in her awareness of that early choice. She is at least mindful of some of the factors in that selection. For most of her people, this is rarely the case. Their treatment is designed to impress them with their lowly position. The role of inferiority into which they have been cast has affected them deeply, but if the wounds are not physical, they are easily ignored.

The American black man is unique, but he has no special psychology or exceptional genetic determinants. His mental mechanisms are the same as other men. If he undergoes emotional conflict, he will respond as neurotically as his white brother. In understanding him we return to the same reference point, since all other explanations fail. We must conclude that much of the pathology we see in black people had its genesis in slavery. The culture that was born in that experience of bondage has been passed from generation to generation. Constricting adaptations developed during some long-ago time continue as contemporary character traits. That they are so little altered attests to the fixity of the black-white relationship, which has seen little change since the birth of this country.

Long ago in the United States basic decisions were made. The most important of these made color the crucial variable. This began as the cornerstone of the system of black slavery. After refinements, it has remained to become imbedded in the national character. Persisting to this day is an attitude, shared by black and white alike, that blacks are inferior. This belief permeates every facet of this country and it is the etiological agent from which has developed the national sickness.

The early farmers who migrated to this country were no more evil than other men. Many had fled from intolerable situations, caste systems, and religious warfare. They came filled with hope. A chance combination offered these early farmers fertile land and slaves. Initially, these slaves may have been black or white or, in the odd case, Indian. The country expanded and more and more land became available for cultivation. Supply and demand followed a predictable course and, with blacks available in large numbers, the African remained as the only bondsman.

Generations passed and the white master and the black slave became more dependent on each other economically and psychologically. Their lives took on a symbiotic quality. When eventually the white assumed absolute power over the black, the psychology of each was changed. The reasoning which allowed these atrocities infused itself into the national thought. To hide and rationalize the barbarism, the justification became national in scope. All Americans were not slaveholders, but until a short while ago this was essentially a nation of farmers. A man working a harsh land knows that one uses whatever tools are available and he would not criticize his neighbor who held slaves.

The early white Americans were free of English common law. They were not a colony as was Brazil, subject to the laws of a European country with a long tradition of dealing with slaves. There were no powerful clerics, such as in the Catholic Church, to insist that slaves had rights. And with a burgeoning economy, everyone was willing to continue any practice which might bring more goods into the marketplace.

The nation became involved in a bizarre system of reasoning about slaves. No longer were they simply unfortunate beings caught up in an economic system which exploited their labor. Now they were to be subhuman—quasi-humans who not only preferred slavery but felt it best for them. The American had to hide from himself and others his oppression of blacks. To be safe, the entire country had to share in the denial.

In the second half of the twentieth century the posture of the nation generally is only slightly changed. Long after slavery, many whites are haunted by a vision of being oppressed, exposed to the whims of a powerful cruel *black* man. To dissipate the fantasy, increasing barriers have had to be erected. In reality it seems a remote possibility that blacks might overthrow their oppressors and enslave them. But all men have the capacity to deceive themselves, and the entire country has participated in devising humiliating laws and customs. Pseudo-scientific theories of racial superiority have been elaborated and unreasoning fears of blacks have become a part of the national character. How else to explain such massive preparations for such an unlikely attack?

An ex-serviceman recalled an incident. During World War II he was stationed in rural Montana. On a weekend he visited a nearby town. When he arrived he was the object of much wonder. No one in town had ever seen a black man before.

He went into a restaurant. The manager was polite and friendly. He passed the time of day and allowed as how this was the first Negro he had ever laid eyes on. He talked about the town and the generous nature of its people and then told the unfortunate brother that the restaurant had a policy against serving Negroes.

White citizens have grown up with the identity of an American and, with that, the unresolved conflicts of the slaveholder. White Americans are born into a culture which contains the hatred of blacks as an integral part.

Blacks are no longer the economic underpinnings of the nation. But they continue to be available as victims and therefore a ready object for the projection of hostile feelings. Throughout the country they are highly visible, by now useless for exploitation, and demanding participation in the affairs of the country.

Because there has been so little change in attitudes, the children of bondage continue to suffer the effects of slavery. There is a timeless quality to the unconscious which transforms yesterday into today. The obsessions of slave and master continue. Both continue a deadly struggle of which neither is fully aware. It would seem that for most black people emancipation has yet to come.

A harried young mother, having exhausted the resources of several social agencies, turned to the psychiatrist as a last resort.

She had a pretty face but she was obese and wore frazzled clothes. As a result, she looked like a shapeless, middle-aged woman. On the first visit she wore an ill-fitting red wig which fell forward over her eyes. She made motions to right it, only to have it lodge over her ears.

She told of her difficulties by describing various crises. The younger children were sick and two older boys had disappeared the previous evening. A riot had broken out on that same evening and she feared for the safety of her sons.

She lived with her five children in a rat-infested apartment. She had never been married and most of her twenty-six years had been spent in public housing projects, living on welfare grants. With five children, she ran out of money near the middle of the month. Then her mother, who could scarcely afford it, would help her buy food. If the groceries were paid for, her roof would begin leaking, and once again she would call the housing office, only to be insulted.

The final blow involved problems with a "raunchy nigger." He had lived with her for several months and had disappeared when the last welfare check was late.

The most bitter outburst was reserved for the Welfare Department. It was headed by a "boss man" who, she believed, found delight in harassing black women. No one had any privacy. The woman next door awakened in the middle of the night, trembling with fright, to discover that the noise at the window was a social worker peering in to determine if a man was sleeping there.

The patient despised public charity, but having stopped school after the ninth grade, she found her meager skills of little use. Some of her neighbors worked as domestics, but only those with few or no children. If a woman had more than two young children, she could not earn enough to pay a sitter. On and on she went. Through most of her narrative she maintained her composure. But as she was relating an incident of little consequence, the tears came and, as she wept, her strength was revealed.

She continued to talk of her life and its burdens. In a short lifetime she had been subjected to great suffering, but she was not defeated. With genuine humor she could acknowledge and laugh at her shortcomings. In the midst of tears, she became warm and chuckled as she related an incident about her children. Hidden in the despair was a distinctive vitality. It came out when she told of her church work or a meeting with a friend. As she spoke, her natural generosity was apparent.

At the end of the hour she dried her eyes, rearranged her wig, and strode out. As she moved, a particular style came through. She was depressed, upset, angry, and had ner share of problems. She moved slowly, but her head was high. She disappeared down the hall. One knew that in the agony of her life was the beauty and torment of the black experience in this country.

If the resources and imperfections of this young woman were unique to her, her story would not assume such importance. Familiar concepts could adequately describe her intrapsychic conflict. We would search her past for early trauma, distorted relationships, and infantile conflicts. The social milieu from which she came would be considered but would not be given much weight. Our youthful subject, however, is black and this one fact transcends all others.

She perceives herself and her surroundings in a manner deeply influenced by this fact. The dismal quality of her life shows how little society thinks of her. Six generations have passed since slavery, and her view of life's possibilities is the same as that of a slave on a Georgia plantation. The reluctant conclusion is that her assets and liabilities are the same as that slave's. She is wily, resourceful, and practiced in the art of survival. But, like her "soul sister" in bondage, she is a victim from the time of her birth. This society has placed her at a disadvantage from which she cannot recover. However visible her deficiencies, the true burdens are subtle and strike at her soul. For the more we become immersed in her problems, the more her life spells out a tragedy.

She meets her problems with ordinary defenses. But *her* difficulties have existed for hundreds of years. The pathology she shows is common to most Negroes. The curbing of her aggression began at an early age. It was in large measure determined by a society that is frightened of her. Beneath her passivity lies anger which might otherwise be directed at white people. As a consequence, we see the dependency about which so much has been written. This is another legacy of slavery. In the morning of her life, she saw her mother and other black adults vulnerable to the whim of white persons. From this it would seem logical that she could become as helpless in this society as her enslaved ancestors. To be prevented from growing and maturing is to be kept in a state of dependency.

The means by which she controls her anger have a direct link to the silent war between master and slave. She must be cautious. This may be why she speaks of the "boss man" with such bitterness. She sees him as free to hurt her, while she can never act on her hate for him. That they are both trapped in such an unequal contest is again a tribute to the unchanging nature of America.

In meeting the world, she seems defensive, as if protecting herself from a thousand slights. Her armor, however, guards against real danger. The suspiciousness may seem excessive, but to relax can be to invite disaster. If these types of character traits are seldom encountered in whites, it is because they do not face the same assaults or grow up in the same climate of hatred. As a result, this woman exhibits emotional weariness. The reality of being alternately attacked, ignored, then singled out for some cruel and undeserved punishment must extract its toll. That penalty may be a premature aging and an early death in some black people. To be regarded always as subhuman is a stultifying experience.

It is people like our patient whom the nation now

fears. Some feel that she threatens the basic social structure. There is a dread that Negroes will impoverish the country by proliferating on welfare rolls. Recently there has been a fear that they will gain political control of the cities now that whites are fleeing to the suburbs. No one can doubt that white America is afraid.

If our black woman could wipe away the tears, she would laugh. Reflect if you will: the most powerful nation on earth, afraid of the poorest, least educated, most leaderless ten percent of its population. Truly the white American projects his own hostility onto the latter-day slave. How else to understand his terror?

Our young patient weeps for good reason. She has seen her hopes soar only to be frustrated. But where her parents retreated into their black world, she is now demanding more of the white man's world. After three centuries of oppression, along with other black people, she has made a vow.

*I will take it no longer.*

We weep for the true victim, the black American. His wounds are deep. But along with their scars, black people have a secret. Their genius is that they have survived. In their adaptations they have developed a vigorous style of life. It has touched religion, music, and the broad canvas of creativity. The psyche of black men has been distorted, but out of that deformity has risen a majesty. It began in the chants of the first work song. It continues in the timelessness of the blues. For white America to understand the life of the black man, it must recognize that so much time has passed and so little has changed.

# III

# *Achieving Womanhood*

In the world of women an abundance of feminine narcissism is not only a cheerful attribute but a vital necessity to emotional well-being. For a woman to invite and accept the love of a man whom she respects, she must feel herself to be eminently worthy of his interest and, in a deep and abiding sense, a lovable person. Such a conviction carries with it a compelling confidence grown out of the loving engagement of a mother with her precious child, of a family with a delightful little girl, and of a larger community likewise charmed by her. With these benevolent auspices, augmented by real physical attractiveness, the stage is set for the growth and development of a self-confident woman who can enter

wholeheartedly into love relationships, bringing a richness and a warmth to her mate and to the children who
issue from their union. The first measure of a child's
worth is made by her mother, and if, as is the case with
so many black people in America, that mother feels that
she herself is a creature of little worth, this daughter, however valued and desired, represents her scorned self. Thus
the girl can be loved and valued only within a limited
sphere, and can never be the flawless child, because she
is who she is—black and inevitably linked to her black,
depreciated mother—always seen to be lacking, deficient,
and faulty in some way. Nor can the family or the community at large undo this attitude, since children, however wonderful they may be to adults, are always seen in
terms of the future, and in this country the future of a
dark girl is dark indeed. While under other circumstances a golden future might be imagined for her, at
the very beginning of her life she is comforted and
commiserated with and urged to overcome her handi-
caps—the handicap of being born black.

A certain amount of feminine narcissism must rest
ultimately on real physical attractiveness and such attractiveness is determined by the artificial standard each
community selects. In this country, the standard is the
blond, blue-eyed, white-skinned girl with regular features.
Since communication media spread this ideal to every
inhabitant of the land via television, newspapers, maga-
zines, and motion pictures, there is not much room for
deviation. Women expend great effort in bringing themselves to an approximation of the ideal. The girl who is
black has no option in the matter of how much she will

change herself. Her blackness is the antithesis of a creamy white skin, her lips are thick, her hair is kinky and short. She is, in fact, the antithesis of American beauty. However beautiful she might be in a different setting with different standards, in this country she is ugly. However loved and prized she may be by her mother, family, and community, she has no real basis of feminine attractiveness on which to build a sound feminine narcissism. When to her physical unattractiveness is added a discouraging, depreciating mother-family-community environment into which she is born, there can be no doubt that she will develop a damaged self-concept and an impairment of her feminine narcissism which will have profound consequences for her character development.

In addition, she takes her place within a historical context, in which women like her have never been valued, have been viewed only as depreciated sexual objects who serve as the recipients of certain debased passions of men who are ashamed to act them out with their own women. Historically she has had some value as a "breeder" of slaves and workmen. But most of all she has been viewed, as all black people have been viewed, as a source of labor: and she has been valued for the amount of work she can perform.

Born thus, depreciated by her own kind, judged grotesque by her society, and valued only as a sexually convenient laboring animal, the black girl has the disheartening prospect of a life in which the cards are stacked against her and the achievement of a healthy, mature womanhood seems a very long shot indeed. The miracle is that, in spite of such odds, the exceptional love of parents and the exceptional strength of many girls produce so many healthy, capable black women.

One aspect of the black woman's life which attracts little attention from outsiders has to do with her hair. From the time of her birth, the little girl must submit to efforts aimed at changing the appearance of her hair. When she is a babe in arms her hair is brushed and stroked, but in short order the gentle brushing gives way to more vigorous brushing and ultimately combing. Her hair is kinky and combing is painful, but her mother must hold her and force her to submit to it. As far back as her memory will take her, the black woman recalls the painful daily ritual of having her hair combed. It is not insignificant that this painful process is administered in a dispassionate way by the mother. Surely the deadly logic of children would try to explain this phenomenon in some such fashion: "If such pain is administered with such regularity by one who purports to love me, then the end result must be extremely important." And yet, however she might search, the child will never find a reason weighty enough to justify the pain to which she must submit.

For, in fact, the combing and plaiting of the hair, in whatever stylish manner the mother may adopt, results only in the child's being rendered "acceptable." The combing does not produce a stunningly beautiful child from an ugly one, but simply an acceptably groomed child. For the pain she goes through, she might well expect to be stopped on the street by strangers stunned by the beauty and the transformation wrought by the combing and the stylized plaits. Not so. She is simply considered to be of an acceptable appearance.

Again, the logic of children would raise the question: 'If Mother has to inflict such pain on me to bring me to the level of acceptability, then I must have been ugly indeed before the combing." For the implications and regularity and torture involved suggest that it is of vital importance that the child not be seen in her "natural state."

Now there is nothing unique about grooming being painful for children. In fact, most people of the soap-and-water cultures may recall the agonies experienced as children when soap got in their eyes. But for most people the discomforts associated with soap, toothbrushes, combs, and slippery bathtubs are transient, experienced mainly by the child who has not quite mastered the technique. It takes only a few years to take most of the pain out of the use of soap and most of the danger out of slippery bathtubs. But for the black girl the combing continues as a daily ritual up to the magic day when she is introduced to the hairdresser.

At the time of this writing the overwhelming majority of Negro women have their hair "fixed" by some method, including the use of a hot comb. The hair is oiled and the heated comb is applied. Usually there is some incidental burning of the scalp. The ordeal itself is long and tiresome, involving hours spent waiting while the overworked beautician moves from customer to customer. To look "presentable" the woman must have her hair pressed every week, or at least every two weeks. Thus the black woman is never free of the painful reminder that she must be transformed from her natural state to some other state in order to appear presentable to her fellow men.

One might ask how this process differs from the ritual to which her Caucasian sister submits for the purpose of similar cosmetic effect. The difference may be a fine one, but it is crucial. The Caucasian woman can brush her hair with a minimum of discomfort and look quite acceptable for any public appearance. If she submits to the pain and discomfort of the hairdresser's, it is for the purpose of *beautification*—it is to enhance her natural appearance which in itself is considered acceptable by her peers. For black women, the pressing comb is like the curse of Eve, a painful, humiliating experience to which she is bound to submit—which, moreover, seems like a wretched legacy grafted into her flesh by her mother.

Almost without exception black women in treatment recall that awful day when they first faced the swimming pool. The black woman's white companions with or without swimming caps plunged into the pool while she stood trembling on the edge, sure that her swimming cap would not fit tightly enough and that afterward she would remove her cap to find disaster.

Women recall the first few weeks at boarding school or college when the issue of having their hair pressed loomed so large. These recollections take on a humorous quality, but the humor is bitter. And not all of it is humor.

A black woman in treatment, who was a borderline schizophrenic, dreaded going to the beauty parlor. She got upset whenever she went and on occasion a visit would be the precipitating incident of her illness. She became delusional and hallucinated. She was terrified in the beauty parlor and thought that the beauticians were whispering behind her back, plotting to do dreadful things to her, and at the very least engaging in malicious gossip. She was terrified of submitting herself to their care. Her associations were to the painful hair combing administered by her devoted grandmother. In her mind the question was never resolved. Did Grandmother truly take pleasure in hurting her? This woman's weak ego may have allowed her to give voice to the silent puzzlement of her countless healthier sisters.

As if this were not sufficient, there is one final degradation associated with hair. Passionate love-making is a vigorous business and touseled hair is to be expected, but if a woman perspires too freely, her pressed hair becomes kinky and must be straightened. And thus even in the triumphant bed of Eros she is reminded that what should be her crowning glory is in fact a crown of shame.

It is against this endless circle of shame, humiliation, and the implied unacceptability of one's own person that a small but significant number of black women have turned to the "natural hairdo"; no hot irons, no pressing combs, no oils, but a soft, black, gentle cloche of cropped velvet. The effect is so engaging and feminine, and, in light of the above, so psychologically redemptive, that we can only wonder why it has taken them so long, and why even yet there are so few.

Publications designed for Negro audiences have always found a certain group of advertisers eager to purchase space. These are the merchants of bleaching creams. The buyers are promised that the cream will make them "two or three shades lighter." The advertising space and the prominent display of these items in neighborhood stores provide objective evidence of what every ghetto dweller knows. Black women have spent fortunes trying to be white.

Long, straight hair and a fair skin have seemed to be the requirements for escaping the misery of being a black woman. One can only guess at the agony of the countless black women who spent their hard-earned money for a bottled, emulsified escape from being the way they are. And it is difficult to imagine their frustration and hopelessness when they finally realized that they could not change their hair or their color.

There surely is nothing more cruelly contained than the feminine narcissism in American black women. To paraphrase Countee Cullen:

> And yet I wonder at this thing
> To make a woman black and bid her sing.

There have been lesser sources of misery too, as if these were not enough. Black women felt ashamed if their feet were big. They hid their feet and bought shoes that were too small and often earned a lifetime of foot problems.

Most cultures associate big feet with lower-class origins and thus the women (and men) value small feet. For the American Negro, "lower class" does not adequately state the condition he wants to rise above. For him, "lower class" has overtones of slavery and the lash, and the black woman's shame when her feet are large is therefore a deeper wound and a more lasting hurt.

They have also felt a special misery over skinny legs and small breasts. In fact, there was a heightened concern over all the criteria of femininity—all the criteria of physical beauty thrust upon them by a society which held beauty to be the opposite of what they were.

The softly seductive, essentially feminine quality of women is at its height during adolescence. In this country great efforts are expended in extending the period, both backward and forward. Backward, to the preadolescence of eleven- and twelve-year-olds, and forward, past the sixties and seventies to the end of a woman's life. Whatever the chronological boundaries, the effort clearly is to extend them and make it possible for a woman to appear more feminine for a longer period of her life.

For a great many black women, however, the process is reversed. Black women seem unconsciously to shorten this period more drastically than their poor circumstances might necessitate. In their thirties and forties they seem to give up competition for male interest. They neglect their figures, allow themselves to become obese, concern themselves more with the utility of their clothing and less with style, and resign themselves to a relatively asexual maternal role in which work and a hovering concern for the family occupies them entirely. They give the impression that they have no interest in men in a sexual way. The total effect such women give can be startling.

A group of relatively poor black mothers who were seen in therapy appeared at first glance to be in their forties or fifties. They were, however, all in their late twenties. Their shapeless garments, unattractive shoes, dental neglect, and general disinterest in their appearance made them seem twenty to thirty years older than they actually were.

A similar disinterest in physical appearance may be noticed in their white counterparts, but the careful observer will see a sharper, chronologically earlier, and a much more widespread relinquishment of youth on the part of black women.

The abandonment of youthful narcissism and the associated competition for male attention can occur at even earlier ages, and in fact may begin at such an early age as to subvert even the high-spirited period of adolescence.

Those who deal with the problems of adolescence are concerned about the high frequency of obesity in Negro girls. The authors are well aware that obesity is a problem of adolescence for young girls of every ethnic origin in the United States. But statistics seem to show that obesity is very much more frequent among black girls. It is also well known that women and mothers who find themselves heavily burdened with problems of day-to-day management and survival find it difficult to expend much energy on feminine frills and finery. But the incidence of abandonment of feminine adornment and narcissistic interest is much greater among black women and is not a direct function of their poverty or disadvantaged circumstances. In fact, however slow has been the movement of black people as a group toward greater advantages, a small rise in income lifts the burden of black women to a very significant degree.

Only a short time ago her task as a home maker was prodigious; home appliances are relatively recent luxuries. One would think, therefore, that she would now have more time and more energy to devote to her own person and to the pleasures of femininity. But the whole issue of work and responsibility has no place in any attempt to explain the obesity and the associated abandonment of sexual competition by adolescent black girls.

If this surrender cuts across all age groups, one must look for other reasons. The most satisfactory explanation would be that femininity is only imperfectly grasped by most black women in any event, since femininity in this society is defined in such terms that it is out of reach for her. If the society says that to be attractive is to be white, she finds herself unwittingly striving to be something she cannot possibly be; and if femininity is rooted in feeling oneself eminently lovable, then a society which views her as unattractive and repellent has also denied her this fundamental wellspring of femininity.

So it may be that after a brief struggle a black woman feels that femininity, as it is defined in these times, is something she cannot achieve. Rather than having her heart broken every day, she relinquishes the struggle and diverts her interest elsewhere. She has derived none of the intensely personal satisfaction she might have received as an honored and desirable sexual object.

There is another factor in her ready rejection of youth and it has deep historical roots. It has been said that beauty is a curse to a subject woman. From the time black people arrived in this country up to the very recent years black women have been sexually available to any white man who felt so inclined. They were not protected by the laws and their men stood in jeopardy of life if a hand was raised in their defense. For the slave or subject woman, youth and beauty meant arousing the interest of the oppressor and exposure to sexual exploitation.

The black girl found herself in a peculiar vise. If her dreams were realized and she grew into a beauty, her problems were far from solved and had in fact only begun. She now attracted the attention of the oppressor, who turned her femininity to the service of his own sexual appetite.

Thus youth and beauty, though desired, were also dreaded as the certain bearer of trouble and strife.

Even now, the pressures on the pretty girl of the ghetto are great and it requires a special heroism for her to avoid the identity of an anonymous sexual object.

Small wonder that black women flee the beauty of youth.

Much of our discussion has dealt with feminine narcissism from a genetic, dynamic, and adaptive point of view. But the perception of oneself in a favorable light includes the identification of oneself in a historical, sequential sense as well. Group identity and the gathering to oneself of the joys and sufferings of one's forebears play an important part in the construction of a self-identity. The United States presents to all its citizens, but most vividly to the black woman, a negative as well as a positive ideal. The positive ideal, as mentioned above, is in many ways unobtainable for her, inasmuch as it really involves trying to become less Negro and more white. She must be clean, neat, modest, subdued, with hair straightened and hopefully with skin lightened. The negative ideal or paradigm is the black, slovenly, obese, dirty, promiscuous woman. But of all the words, perhaps the most important are those that designate the black woman as ugly and repellent. Of the two forces moving her, the pull and attraction of the positive ideal and the push and repulsion of the negative, the latter is by far the more powerful.

Her situation is made worse by the fact that she can by no means approximate the positive ideal and feels always in danger of finding herself too close to the negative. Moreover, the central position of feminine narcissism in the development of character presents a problem for the black woman in her evaluation of her intelligence. Intellectual achievement is closely linked to healthy narcissism. With an impairment of narcissism, a sound synthesis of intellectual accomplishment within the character structure is difficult to achieve.

The full flowering of a woman's sexual function and her capacity to enjoy it are based on her evaluation of herself. If she considers herself an especially worthwhile person, she can joyfully submit to her lover, knowing that he will likewise prize and value her. Her enjoyment of the sexual function will not be impaired by the feeling of being degraded by the man. There is, however, a more subtle interaction between narcissism and the sexual function in women. There is a natural inclination for a woman to yield herself to a powerful lover, gaining additional narcissistic supplies in her possession of him. Her own high evaluation of herself, in turn, evokes in the man a similar high evaluation of her. If her narcissism is impaired, the sexual act is a degrading submission to a man who does not value her, and she arises from it feeling a loss of self-esteem rather than a personal enhancement.

The Negro woman's black face, African features, and kinky hair are physical attributes which place her far from the American ideal of beauty, and make her, with reference to the American ideal, ugly. When the feeling of ugliness is reinforced by the rejection of family and society, the growing girl develops a feeling not only of being undesirable and unwanted but also of being mutilated—of having been fashioned by Nature in an ill-favored manner. Anatomy determines that every little girl will struggle with feelings of having been injured and mutilated when she compares her sexual organs with the male's, but under normal circumstances the compensatory blossoming of narcissism allows her to develop a feeling of satisfaction with herself. The black woman's feelings of mutilation, both psychical and physical, are strengthened by her experiences and she is guarded from self-depreciation only by an enfeebled narcissism. As a result, her personal ambitions as an adolescent and her capacity to live out her aspirations suffer. Under the sign of discouragement and rejection which governs so much of her physical operation, she is inclined to organize her personal ambitions in terms of her achievements and to find these achievements serving to compensate for other losses and hurts.

A dark woman who had risen rapidly in her profession experienced a worsening of her chronic depression. As her achievements grew she found opportunistic men taking an interest in her. She developed intense feelings of bitterness about her job, which she felt was the only element in her attractiveness to men. She was bitter about her intellect which had brought her to her present position. She now was attractive to men who were shallow, opportunistic fortune seekers. To compound her misery, she felt an inclination to accept even these shallow men for whatever they wanted in her.

In choosing a mate, the black woman is again faced with the undesirability of her blackness and with the fact that it is the rare black man who can resist the omnipresent presentation of the white ideal. The compromises that are necessary in the establishment of any relationship between a man and a woman can easily be felt by her to be profound compromises with her own aspirations for a love relationship. She may feel that the compromises are based, not on the difficulties faced by two quite different individuals in adjusting to an intimate union, but on the fact that her "unattractiveness" makes it impossible for her to obtain the "ideal" man.

Thus, the contemporary implications of her Negro-ness and the historical identity it imposes on her make her progress to healthy womanhood much more difficult. The problems we have spelled out here represent barriers which are high but not insurmountable. Because we also see evidence of the remarkable capacity of black people in America to survive, we see one of the adaptive modes chosen by black women to make their way in a hostile world. With youthful narcissism crushed and sexual life perverted, they drew back from these modes as primary means of life expression. Letting youth go, beauty go, and sex go, they narrowed their vision to the most essential feminine function—mothering, nurturing, and protecting their children. In such a role the black woman has been the salvation of many a family. To call such a family matriarchal, as many have done, is to obscure the essential maternal function and to suggest an authoritarian for authority's sake.

We suggest that the black woman has been beset by cruelty on all sides and as a result centered her concern on the most essential quality of womanhood. In so doing she stood by her mate or in his stead when he was crippled or crushed by the oppressor.

The mother in the play *Raisin in the Sun*—who stands as a bulwark of reason between her family and an irrational world—reflects the perception by black women of that essential female function of mothering and its triumph in a world which robs her of other joys.

So much of black women's suffering has grown out of the same feeling of helplessness that has pilloried the male. With the new black movements under way, all that we have just said may assume merely historical significance. The contorted efforts to be white, the shame of the black body, the rejection of youth—may all vanish quickly. Negro women need only see that, truly, "black is beautiful."

# ❮ IV ❯

# *Acquiring Manhood*

## Jimmy

Jimmy was a twelve-year-old boy whose rapid growth had left him gawky and unco    table. He sat slumped in a chair, trying to conceal his ill-fitting clothes. His face was jet-black, and his expressions ranged from somber to sad. Whether relating stories of home, school, or the streets, he disguised his true feelings. At twelve he had learned one of his first lessons—always play it cool. As much as possible, he worked to hide his inner life.

One day he stared long and hard at his fist and said: "I want to hit a white man." For once, the therapist could sense an uncensored outpouring of feelings. Then Jimmy frowned, started another sentence, and began to cry.

The anger was welcome, if unexpected, but the comment was surprising. In over three months of weekly visits, the boy had never directly mentioned white people. There had been allusions to trouble at school with boys who were not "bloods" and once he talked of his father's job at a can factory, where there were few Negroes. But Jimmy had never spoken in terms of racial feelings or problems. He had never directly felt antagonism from a white person, but when his anger spilled over, he chose that target.

He was a quiet, introverted boy who found it difficult to talk for fifty minutes. He would smile in acknowledging something pleasant, but generally he seemed to feel despair. His emotions were expressed in terms of stubbornness and obstinacy. If he felt threatened, he became passive and silent and in this manner opposed anything he did not want to do or say. This was his means of dealing with any authority, whether a teacher in school or a parent. Though he had an above-average intelligence, he was doing poorly in school. There were important things he would not do or forgot to do, and his grades suffered. In talking about his life, Jimmy was vague. He had trouble seeing anything in his life as definite, with any form or shape.

One thing in his life was clear. He saw his father as weak and powerless. However much his father threatened, cajoled, or beat him, Jimmy always knew that the man was playing a role.

His father was a large man, lighter in color than his son, and grossly overweight. He dressed in rumpled suits, wrinkled shirts, and greasy ties. In some of the early family sessions, he would interrupt to complain of his various ailments. He spoke of an ulcer that was always "acting up." Mr. B. "played at" (this was Jimmy's phrase) being the minister of a storefront church, in addition to his full-time job at the factory. From an early age, Jimmy was aware that his father could never "stand up." He had heard his mother say it and he observed it himself. One of the boy's few delights was in recalling an occasion when his father cringed and sent his wife to the door to handle a bill collector. Many of Jimmy's friends did not have their fathers living at home, but he was certain that those fathers, in the same situation, would have acted the same way.

Mrs. B. was a short, dark woman with an attractive but worried face. She was neat and "fixed up" and openly compared her appearance with her husband's usually disheveled state. She did not hide her contempt for him. She constantly undermined his feeble attempts to relate to Jimmy. She was the dominant figure in the house, and she assumed this position as an unwanted burden, as something about which she had no choice. She would alternate between understanding Jimmy and dramatically washing her hands of everything.

In terms of individual psychopathology, Jimmy can be matched with thousands of teenage boys of every race and ethnic background.   is responding to his puberty with restlessness and feelings he cannot articulate directly. He is angry with his father and alternately attracted to and repelled by his mother. Every therapist has seen many Jimmys. What is different about him is that he is black and is experiencing what every black boy in this country must undergo. His personality and character structure, his emotional assets and liabilities, are being shaped as much by his blackness as by his personal environment.

Jimmy is beginning to realize that he has no power and, like his father, will not get it. At his age the concepts are misty, but he realizes that his father and the fathers of his friends are lacking something. He has had few, if any, traumatic incidents with whites. There have been no overt acts of discrimination. The family has lived in a ghetto, and all their socialization has been within that framework. But Jimmy is part of a historical legacy that spans more than three hundred years. He lives in a large city but he shares his insight with every black child in every city in this country. He must devise individual ways to meet group problems. He must find compensations, whether healthy or unhealthy. There must be a tremendous expenditure of psychic energy to cushion the shock of learning that he is denied what other men around him have. When he states his desire to attack a white man, he consciously acknowledges his wish to attack those who keep him powerless.

Both theories of personality development and clinical experience attest to the troubled path from childhood to manhood. The young man must have developed a fine expertise in making his way in a complex and ambiguous social organization. Under the most favorable signs it is a difficult task and society must turn its most benign and helping face to the young aspirant. And once the game is mastered a certain flexible readiness is required because the rules are constantly being changed.

Thus the black boy in growing up encounters some strange impediments. Schools discourage his ambitions, training for valued skills is not available to him, and when he does triumph in some youthful competition he receives compromised praise, not the glory he might expect. In time he comes to see that society has locked arms *against* him, that rather than help he can expect opposition to his development, and that he lives not in a benign community but in a society that views his growth with hostility.

For the black man in this country, it is not so much a matter of acquiring manhood as it is a struggle to feel it his own. Whereas the white man regards his manhood as an ordained right, the black man is engaged in a never-ending battle for its possession. For the black man, attaining any portion of manhood is an active process. He must penetrate barriers and overcome opposition in order to assume a masculine posture. For the inner psychological obstacles to manhood are never so formidable as the impediments woven into American society. By contrast, for a white man in this country, the rudiments of manhood are settled at birth by the possession of a penis and a white skin. This biological affirmation of masculinity and identity as master is enough to insure that, whatever his individual limitations, this society will not systematically erect obstructions to ' ' achievement.

Throughout his life, a ach critical point of development the black boy is told to hold back, to constrict, to subvert and camouflage his normal masculinity. Male assertiveness becomes a forbidden fruit, and if it is attained, it must be savored privately.

Manhood must always be defined for the setting in which it occurs. A man in a Siberian village may be very different from a man in a Chicago suburb. Biologically they share the same drives and limitations, but their societies may decree totally different roles. Manhood in this country has many meanings, but a central theme is clear. Men are very early taught that they have certain prerogatives and privileges. They are encouraged to pursue, to engage life, to attack, rather than to shrink back. They learn early that to express a certain amount of aggression and assertion is manly. Every playground, every schoolyard is filled with boys fighting and attacking, playing at being grown up. The popular heroes in this country are men who express themselves aggressively and assertively.

As boys approach adulthood, masculinity becomes more and more bound up with money making. In a capitalistic society economic wealth is inextricably interwoven with manhood. Closely allied is power—power to control and direct other men, power to influence the course of one's own and other lives. The more lives one can influence, the greater the power. The ultimate power is the freedom to understand and alter one's life. It is this power, both individually and collectively, which has been denied the black man.

Under slavery, the black man was a psychologically emasculated and totally dependent human being. Times and conditions have changed, but black men continue to exhibit the inhibitions and psychopathology that had their genesis in the slave experience. It would seem that for masculine growth and development the psychological conditions have not changed very much. Better jobs are available, housing is improving, and all the external signs of progress can be seen, but the American heritage of racism will still not allow the black man to feel himself master in his own land. Just as Jimmy is beset by forces larger than his individual experiences, so is the black man in this society, more than other men, shaped by currents more powerful than the course of his own life. There are rules which regulate black lives far more than the lives of white men.

The simplistic view of the black family as a matriarchy is an unfortunate theme repeated too often by scholars who should know better. If a man is stripped of his authority in the home by forces outside that home, the woman naturally must assume the status of head of household. This is the safety factor inherent in a household which includes two adults and it by no means suggests that the woman prefers it that way. If a woman is widowed she may assume many masculine functions, but the household may be a patriarchy without a patriarch.

In the black household the man faces greater than usual odds in making his way. The care and rearing of children falls even more heavily on the wife; she is the culture bearer. She interprets the society to the children and takes as her task the shaping of their character to meet the world as she knows it. This is every mother's task. But the black mother has a more ominous message for her child and feels more urgently the need to get the message across. The child must know that the white world is dangerous and that if he does not understand its rules it may kill him.

When black men recall their early life, consistent themes emerge. For example, the mother is generally perceived as having been sharply contradictory. She may have been permissive in some areas and punitive and rigid in others. There are remembrances of stimulation and gratification coexisting with memories of deprivation and rejection. There is always a feeling that the behavior of the mother was purposeful and deliberate.

The black man remembers that his mother underwent frequent and rapid shifts of mood. He remembers the cruelty. The mother who sang spirituals gently at church was capable of inflicting senseless pain at home. These themes of gratification and cruelty are consistent enough to suggest that they played a critical role in preparing the boy for adulthood. It would seem that the boy had to experience the polarities of ambivalence so that he could understand his later role in a white society. He must be adequately prepared.

The black mother shares a burden with her soul sisters of three centuries ago. She must produce and shape and mold a unique type of man. She must intuitively cut off and blunt his masculine assertiveness and aggression lest these put the boy's life in jeopardy.

During slavery the danger was real. A slave boy could not show too much aggression. The feelings of anger and frustration which channeled themselves into aggression had to be thwarted. If they were not, the boy would have little or no use as a slave and would be slain. If any feelings, especially those of assertive manhood, were expressed too strongly, then that slave was a threat, not only to himself and his master but to the entire system as well. For that, he would have to be killed.

The black mother continues this heritage from slavery and simultaneously reflects the world she now knows. Even today, the black man cannot become too aggressive without hazard to himself. To do so is to challenge the delicate balance of a complex social system. Every mother, of whatever color and degree of proficiency, knows what the society in which she lives will require of her children. Her basic job is to prepare the child for this. Because of the institutionalization of barriers, the black mother knows even more surely what society requires of *her* children. What at first seemed a random pattern of mothering has gradually assumed a definite and deliberate, if unconscious, method of preparing a black boy for his subordinate place in the world.

As a result, black men develop considerable hostility toward black women as the inhibiting instruments of an oppressive system. The woman has more power, more accessibility into the system, and therefore she is more feared, while at the same time envied. And it is her lot in life to suppress masculine assertiveness in her sons.

Mr. R. was a writer who presented himself for treatment in his mid-fifties. In his younger days he had enjoyed success and a certain amount of adulation in white society. Throughout the course of treatment he presented a picture of culture and refinement. His trouble was that several years earlier he had lost the spark of creativity and his writing ceased. He made frequent resolutions to resume writing, but his motivation never matched his ambition.

It developed that he was afraid to compete with white men as a writer. Whatever he wrote, his obsessional fears dictated that somewhere someone who was white had written something better. He was a defeated and despairing man when he entered treatment. He had, however, a delicious secret which he used as comfort when he was most depressed.

His face would crease with a smile when he recounted his numerous affairs as a young man. In all his life he never doubted his ability to outperform a white man sexually. He told how he had "banged many white women." He sometimes spoke of himself as a deformed man or as a cripple, but sex was the one area in which he felt completely adequate.

The mythology and folklore of black people is filled with tales of sexually prodigious men. Most boys grow up on a steady diet of folk heroes who have distinguished themselves by sexual feats. It is significant that few, if any, of these folk heroes are directing armies or commanding empires. Dreams must in some way reflect reality, and in this country the black man, until quite recently, had not been in positions of power. His wielding of power had been in the privacy of the boudoir.

To be sure, black men have sexual problems. They may have impotence, premature ejaculation, and the entire range of pathology which limits and distorts sexual life. Such ailments have the same dynamic origins in men of all races. But where sex is employed as armament and used as a conscious and deliberate means of defense, it is the black man who chooses this weapon. If he cannot fight the white man openly, he can and does battle him secretly. Recurrently, the pattern evolves of black men using sex as a dagger to be symbolically thrust into the white man.

A black man who was an orderly in a hospital had an eighth-grade education and felt himself inadequate in most endeavors. If called upon to perform a new duty, he would reflect for a moment and feel dumbstruck. One evening an attractive young nurse made seductive overtures to him. At first he was not convinced that she was serious but thought she was playing a game. When he discovered that she meant it, he took her to bed with a vengeance. During the weekly therapy hour he would elaborate and expand on his feats. One central fact became more and more clear. He was able to state very directly that every time he possessed the girl sexually, he was making up for having sat on the back of the bus and having endured numberless humiliations. He was getting revenge for generations of slavery and degradation.

One of the constant themes in black folklore is the bad nigger." It seems that every community has had one or was afraid of having one. They were feared as much by blacks as by whites. In the slave legends there are tales of docile field hands suddenly going berserk. It was a common enough phenomenon to appear in writings of the times and to stimulate the erection of defenses against this violent kind of man.

Today black boys are admonished not to be a "bad nigger." No description need be offered; every black child knows what is meant. They are angry and hostile. They strike fear into everyone with their uncompromising rejection of restraint or inhibition. They may seem at one moment meek and compromised—and in the next a terrifying killer. Because of his experience in this country, every black man harbors a potential bad nigger inside him. He must ignore this inner man. The bad nigger is bad because he has been required to renounce his manhood to save his life. The more one approaches the American ideal of respectability, the more this hostility must be repressed. The bad nigger is a defiant nigger, a reminder of what manhood could be.

Cultural stereotypes of the savage rapist-Negro express the fear that the black man will turn on his tormentors. Negro organizations dread the presence of the bad nigger. White merchants who have contact with black people have uneasy feelings when they see a tight mouth, a hard look, and an angry black face. The bad nigger in black men no doubt accounts for more worry in both races than any other single factor.

Granting the limitations of stereotypes, we should nevertheless like to sketch a paradigmatic black man. His characteristics seem so connected to employment that we call it "the postal-clerk syndrome." This man is always described as "nice" by white people. In whatever integrated setting he works, he is the standard against whom other blacks are measured. "If they were all only like him, everything would be so much better." He is passive, nonassertive, and nonaggressive. He has made a virtue of identification with the aggressor, and he has adopted an ingratiating and compliant manner. In public his thoughts and feelings are consciously shaped in the direction he thinks white people want them to be. The pattern begins in childhood when the mother may actually say: "You must be this way because this is the only way you will get along with Mr. Charlie."

This man renounces gratifications that are available to others. He assumes a deferential mask. He is always submissive. He must figure out "the man" but keep "the man" from deciphering him. He is prevalent in the middle and upper-middle classes, but is found throughout the social structure. The more closely allied to the white man, the more complete the picture becomes. He is a direct lineal descendant of the "house nigger" who was designed to identify totally with the white master. The danger he poses to himself and others is great, but only the surface of passivity and compliance is visible. The storm below is hidden.

A leading Negro citizen came to a therapy session with his wife, who was suffering from a severe and intractable melancholia. She had several times seriously attempted suicide. The last attempt was particularly serious. She was angry with her husband and berated him for never opening up and exposing his feelings.

For his part, the husband remained "nice." He never raised his voice above a murmur. His wife could goad him, but he was the epitome of understanding. He was amenable to all suggestions. His manner and gestures were deliberate, studied, and noninflammatory. Everything was under-stated. During the course of treatment he was involved in several civil rights crises. His public life was an extension of his private one, and he used such words as "moderation" and "responsibility." His entire life was a study in passivity, in how to play at being a man without really being one.

It would be easy to write off this man as an isolated passive individual, but his whole community looks upon his career as a success story. He made it in the system to a position of influence and means. And it took an aggres-sive, driving, determined man to make it against the odds he faced. We must ask how much energy is required for him to conceal his drive so thoroughly. And we wonder what would happen if his controls ever failed.

Starting with slavery, black people, and more particularly black men, have had to devise ways of expressing
themselves uniquely and individually and in a manner
that was not threatening to the white man. Some methods
of giving voice to aggressive masculinity have become
institutionalized. The most stylized is the posture of
"playing it cool."

The playing-it-cool style repeats itself over and over
again in all aspects of black life. It is an important
means of expression and is widely copied in the larger
white culture. A man may be overwhelmed with conflict, threatened with an eruption of feelings, and barely
maintaining his composure, but he will present a serene
exterior. He may fear the eruption of repressed feelings
if they bring a loss of control, but an important aspect
of his containment is the fear that his aggression will be
directed against the white world and will bring swift
punishment. The intrapsychic dynamics may be similar
in a white man, but for the black man it is socially far
more important that the façade be maintained.

Patients have come for treatment who have had one
or two visits with a variety of psychiatrists, psychologists,
and social workers. In many cases they were written off
as having no significant pathology or as being "poor
patients." The importance of the cool style is apparent
when one realizes the cost and suffering required to
maintain it. Those who practice it have raised to a high
art a life style which seems a peculiarly black contribution to adaptation in this society.

Several decades ago, observers were impressed by the
black community's adulation of Joe Louis. They were
a starved and deprived group, but, even so, their deifica-

tion of him seemed all out of proportion. In retrospect, there is an explanation. In the ring he was the picture of fury. As he demolished foe after foe, every black man could vicariously taste his victory. If his victims were white, the pleasure was even greater. He symbolized assertiveness and unbridled aggression for the black man. In watching him or reading about him, an entire community could find expression through him of inhibited masculine drives. As others have entered professional sports in later years, the heroes have served a similar purpose. Educated and sophisticated Negroes also participate in this hero worship, since all black men swim in the same sea.

A black man in treatment kept reaching for a memory. He finally recalled watching a fight on television, at a time when a black coed, Authurine Lucey, was integrating the University of Alabama. The contest was between a black and white fighter. During the bout he kept hearing someone shout: "Hit him one for Authurine." Even after he had forgotten the fight, the phrase kept returning to his mind, "Hit him one for Authurine." It became his battle cry. Whenever he was pressed, the thought would come again and again in an obsessional fashion. He then began to talk of his own repressed aggression and the pieces of the puzzle began to fit, and the obsession receded.

When all the repressive forces fail and aggression erupts, it is vital that we ask the right questions. The issue is not what caused the riots of the past few years —that is clear to any man who has eyes. Rather, we must ask: What held this aggression in check for so long and what is the nature of this breached barrier. Dare anyone try to reconstruct it?

During recent riots there was a wry saying in the ghetto. "Chuck can't tell where it's going to hit next because we don't know ourselves." And it was a fact. The most baffling aspect to rioting in Newark, Detroit, and Watts was the complete spontaneity of the violence. Authorities turned to "responsible" Negro leaders to calm the black rebels and the Negro leaders did not know where to start. They were confronted with a leaderless mob which needed no leader. Every man was a leader— they were of one mind.

The goods of America, piled high in the neighborhood stores, had been offered to them with a price tag that made work slavery and made balancing a budget a farce. The pressure was ever on parents to buy a television set, to buy kitchen appliances and new cars. The available jobs paid so poorly and the prices (plus interest) of goods were so high that if one made a purchase he was entering upon years of indebtedness.

The carrot held in front of the ghetto laborer is the consumer item—the auto, the TV, and the hi-fi set. If the poor black man falls into place in America, he takes whatever job is offered, receives minimal pay, purchases hard goods at harder prices, and teeters from insolvency to bankruptcy in the ghetto.

Exhausted, he was offered a stimulant in the form of the civil rights laws. When it became clear that they were nothing more than words from Washington, he kicked over the traces. He took a short cut. Instead of working for a lifetime to buy a piece of slum property which might fall at any moment and which he would likely never own anyway—instead of this treadmill, he burned it down. Instead of working for years to pay three times the usual cost of a television set, he broke a window and stole it. Instead of the desperate, frustrating search to find out which white man was friendly and which was hostile, he simply labeled them all the enemy. There never seemed to be a great deal of difference between friends and enemies anyway. So in a spontaneous blast he burned up the ghetto. And the wrong question continued to be asked: Why a riot in Detroit, where conditions were so good?

The worst slum and the best slum are very close together compared with the distance separating the world of black men and the world of whites. At bottom, America remains a slave country which happens to have removed the slave laws from the books. The question we must ask is: What held the slave rebellion in check for so long?

The racist tradition is pervasive and envelops every American. For black men it constitutes a heavy psychological burden. From the unemployed, illiterate ghetto dweller to the urbanized man living in an integrated setting, careful examination shows psychological scars. Black men fight one another, do violence to property, do hurtful things to themselves while nursing growing hatred for the system which oppresses and humiliates them. Their manhood is tested daily. As one patient expressed it: "The black man in this country fights the main event in Madison Square Garden every day."

A reflective and cautious man relates some episode of irrational and aggressive behavior. He has spent a lifetime suppressing his feelings, and now he is frightened and wants reassurance that what has happened will not recur.

Another man erupts and attacks a neighbor who knocks on his door.

These incidents, like the regular Saturday-night brawls that have been characteristic of the black ghetto, are the short bursts of rage which find broader expression in Watts, Newark, and Detroit.

Many black men show a curious symptom—weeping without feeling. The tears come without warning and may be quite embarrassing. It is seen frequently in our patient population of black men of above-average achievement. We can only speculate on the basis of a small sample, but it would seem that it also occurs, though with less frequency, among black men of lower socioeconomic levels. Clinical experience indicates that the symptom is relatively rare among white men of all classes.

A man watching a football game on television sees a Negro star take the ball on a long downfield run and as he crosses the goal line in triumph the viewer is aware of tears in his eyes.

Another patient recalls attending a civil rights meeting at which Martin Luther King spoke eloquently. He was suddenly aware of tears.

Another man attended a business meeting at which a successful white businessman was being extolled, and as the guest of honor's unbroken series of business triumphs was told, the patient found himself wiping away tears.

Common to all these incidents is a black man passively viewing another man, black or white, triumphant over odds and standing supreme in a moment of personal glory. Further, the patients were struck by the fact that the tears seemed to come of their own accord, unsummoned and unaccompanied by any emotional feeling or any thought which might cause them to weep. The event was too simple: witnessing another triumphant man, and tears, no feelings, no thoughts.

In the course of treatment, attention was focused on the lack of feeling, and the associations which came gradually made it clear that it was important for the viewer not to allow himself feelings. The obvious forbidden feelings were ones of sadness. And for what? For what he might have been. He might have been the victor receiving the roar of the crowd. The tears are for what he might have achieved if he had not been held back. He was held back by some inner command not to excel, not to achieve, not to become outstanding, not to draw attention to himself. Even at the price of achievement, he felt bound to follow a command to remain anonymous.

Once he sees the compelling nature of this inner rule of behavior, he can trace it to his mother. Only she was so concerned with his behavior and she was most concerned that he be modest and self-effacing. And when he sees that his grief is over lost achievement, relinquished at the behest of his mother, he becomes enraged with her. This was the reason he had to suppress all feeling connected with the tears, because it led too directly to his mother as the inhibiting factor in his development.

Upon reaching this point many patients immediately displace the rage onto society, saying they were not inhibited early in life by parents, but later, upon encountering a restrictive and inhibiting social system where the cards were stacked against them. With some patients the first object of their anger was white society and the second the mother, but always the mother was close to the surface. It was her closeness to the symptom which made necessary the inhibition of feeling associated with the tears.

Finally, there comes later a deeper understanding of the mother as a concerned mediator between society and the child. The patient comes to recognize that, while the larger society imposes a harsh inhibition on his development and a threat to any aggressivity, this hostility of society is communicated to him by his mother, whose primary concern is that he survive. For if he does not realize that his aggressiveness puts him in grave danger from society generally, he may *not* survive. With this recognition his hostility toward his mother lessens and is directed toward white society.

This symptom, seen so frequently, is like an isolated sentinel suggesting deeper layers of interaction between impulse and inhibition, individual drive and the stone wall of external reality.

How much of this finds its roots in history? How did the mother come to systematically drive out manliness from her sons under the sign of love? And does our patient weep only for himself?

We are certain that the answers lie in the past.

# V

# *Marriage and Love*

A schoolteacher married a laborer. They worked hard and with economy and planning managed to acquire a home and a car. Children came as planned, but conflict came and grew. The wife wanted a larger home with a yard. The husband resented her demands. He felt that she had no respect for him, that to her he was merely a provider for her endless wishes. She was embarrassed by his poor education. He felt that she and her friends were "phony" and that she was preoccupied with maintaining senseless appearances. Their mutual hostility led to verbal and later physical assaults. Divorce was the result.

This pattern is so common in Negro marriages that it deserves special study, which might shed light on the broader problems of how in America choice of mate and marriage in general is influenced by a person's blackness.

There are voluminous studies describing the economic and social function of Negroes and we feel no necessity to duplicate this work. Rather we shall link the psychological functioning of the individual to his role as a discrete citizen, as an American, as a black man, and as a member of a family. All his possible roles are in a vital way related to his position as a member of a family: as a son, husband, and father. The family is the matrix out of which the inner, uniquely individual man grows; it is this which first offers him vital information about his world. And later it is the source of comfort which will heal him on his return from the wars it prepared him for.

To understand marriage and choice of mate we must understand childhood. Children develop psychologically within the framework supplied by parents and family. For example, if religion occupies a central position in a family, then each child in that family must develop at least partly in response to religion. It must occupy a certain space within his psychological body. He may adopt a pious posture and at least give the appearance of being a devout and faithful believer in the gods of his fathers. Or he may become irreverent and be actively against religion, presenting himself as diametrically opposed to his religious parents. But while differing from them in this important respect he will resemble them in the amount of psychic energy he devotes to religious matters. Or he may ignore religion and to all intents and purposes disengage himself from it altogether. An inspection will reveal, however, that he has displaced his religious concerns onto some seemingly innocuous area where it escapes recognition. He may even have denied himself that displacement, but in his silence one will sense a significant silent area of his psychic life. There will seem to be a vacuum, a hole, and one later may wonder what had been there.

We want to show that issues which were important in childhood, and important to people who in turn were important to the child, must of necessity show themselves as issues which must be taken into account in the child's later adult life.

A minor point may be illustrative. The racial mixture in the background of black people is so varied that it is extremely rare to find two Negroes who have exactly the same brown tones to their skin. There is usually a bit more yellow or red or black that distinguishes seemingly identical skin colors from one another. But these are minor variations on a brown theme and their least deviations are generally of small moment to adults.

The infant's world is so very different in this regard. His mother's body is a vitally important part of his world. Her breasts, her hands, arms, face, are the most important things he sees and touches. She is the first human he recognizes and for a long time in his small life she is the bringer of life.

As he plays with her breast or face, he looks intently, with the myopic vision of a child, at her skin. Its color becomes to him the color of all loving people's skin, and in fact the particular skin tones he sees as a child will ever after evoke emotional overtones based on that intimacy. It is no wonder then that men choose women whose skin tones are closely matched to their mother's, or that in multiple marriages all the wives will have the identical color.

A woman so fair that one had to take her word for it that she was Negro chose a series of deep-black lovers. She clearly seemed first attracted by their color and, although she gave any number of reasons for her choices, there seemed a deeper cause. A dream reminded her of a deep-black "relative," a gentle kindly man with whom she had no kin, but who had befriended her as a fatherless child and toward whom she ever after maintained a deep attachment. As a matter of fact, tracing this relationship brought her to question her conviction that she was "Negro." There was no proof, but there was much to suggest that she was actually a white girl who had been adopted by Negro foster parents and that her natural father had not been a black man as she had grown up be-lieving. Very possibly, her attachment to the dark man not only had determined the color of her lovers but had in fact determined the racial identity she later assumed.

Thus, with women as well, the color of the father or father surrogate may be so intimately linked with the positive aspects of their attachment to him as to determine the color of all future lovers.

At times, the theme "Black is the color of my true love's skin" might become the credo of several genera-tions of a family.

A fair-skinned girl was the first child of a black mother. The father was white. The parents did not marry, however, and the black mother subsequently married a black man. The dark-skinned children who followed made the fair child's life miserable with taunts about her "yellowness." She came to hate her color and indeed to dislike all fair-skinned people. She married a very dark man and warned her daughters that fair-skinned men were deceptive and not to be trusted. They, in turn, married dark men. And though it is not known what message they conveyed to their daughters, the daughters also chose dark husbands.

Color may be significant for one's own deep emotional responses or may come to symbolize virtue or perfidy, but by far the most universal significance color has had among black Americans has been as a symbol of status.

> If you're white, you're right.
> If you're brown, hang around.
> If you're black, get back.

Sadly, even now there is too much truth in this doggerel. Mothers have wanted fair girls for their sons and fair husbands for their daughters. Until very recent times, beauty among Negro girls has been synonymous with fair skin and a minimum of Negroid features. A "good-looking" Negro man has traditionally been a fair-skinned or light-brown man. The issue has been of less importance to men, since male beauty is of less significance in this country. It has played a part, however, in opportunities available for masculine achievement. In many vocational and academic settings opportunities have come more rapidly for the Negro with a lighter hue and straighter hair.

Thus those Negro families which have placed such a premium on light color have had some meager reality to justify their attitude. We should emphasize the meagerness of the justification, however, for the preponderant sources of their desperate dread of blackness have been their own unreasoning self-hatred and their pitiful wish to be white. Such families can often trace their origins back to a slaveowner who gave land to his children by black mothers or who allowed these children to obtain an education that provided them with economic advantages. As a result, the fair-skinned aristocracy among Negroes are families with money, position, and influence—advantages counterbalanced by the terrible burden of a self-hatred so powerful that they can exercise the greatest cruelties on people who remind them that they too are black.

Such families are becoming anomalous and, more important, they are becoming irrelevant. The grand encounter with which this nation is occupied is between the black masses and the white power holders. Fair-skinned dilettantes have earned little consideration.

But permeating the thinking of all Negroes remains the connection between status and beauty and fair skin. If she were typical, the schoolteacher with whose story this chapter opened is probably fairer than her husband, and in fact most Negro couples are likely to show this color difference. The man pursues the woman, the beauty; and the frequency with which Negro men choose women fairer than they attests at least in part to the connection in the mind of the black man between fair skin and beauty. If in affairs of love women were the aggressors, the color relationship might be reversed.

These are some of the additional considerations that enter into a relationship between a black man and a black woman. Their love and their union produce a family, a new entity. Central to the new union is their adulthood. A marriage signifies the maturity of the partners and, importantly as well, their autonomy. Small wonder that young black married couples are likely to guard their dignity. Honor becomes more important and humiliation more unbearable, not only because the people are young and new at marriage but because it is precisely the perquisites of maturity that are so mindlessly made difficult for black people to enjoy. In such a cruel way it is necessary for each young black man to find his own variety of manhood with which he can live and which does not jeopardize his own safety or that of his now extended self, his wife and children. And the woman must find a way for a flowering of her womanhood which complements her mate and at the same time can bloom in spite of the economic burden she must bear—and in such a way that it does not spur her mate to challenges which jeopardize the family.

The tragedy and complexity of the situation become more apparent when we remember that a family is a functional unit designed for one primary purpose—the protection of the young; and while it serves other vital social purposes, none is more important than the function of *protection*.

But the black family cannot protect its members. Nowhere in the United States can the black family extend an umbrella of protection over its members in the way that a white family can. In every part of the nation its members are subjected to physical and verbal abuse, humiliation, unlawful search and seizure, and harassment by authorities. Its members are jailed, beaten, robbed, killed, and raped, and exposed to this kind of jeopardy to a degree unheard of in white families. Thus the black family is prevented from performing its most essential function—its *raison d'être*—protection of its members.

Marriage among slaves was a farce, but not because of their low station or ignorance of the ways of the nation. It was so because there could be no marriage where the nation moved monolithically and institutionally to keep all slaves exposed to capricious punishment and when by law no man in the nation could protect a slave, least of all the members of his family. By law no slave husband could protect his wife from physical or sexual abuse at the hands of a white man. By law no slave mother could protect her child against physical or sexual abuse at the hands of a white man. These were the reasons why marriage among slaves was meaningless. There could be no functioning family.

All black families in the United States face the task of establishing a family in a nation that is institutionally opposed to this fundamental function of the family. Black husbands cannot provide their wives with as much protection as can white husbands. This can be seen with great clarity in many parts of the South and as one observes the relationship between blacks and policemen in any part of the country. Mothers cannot protect their children from exposure to criminal elements in their neighborhoods because white law-enforcement authorities show little enthusiasm and even less capability for the suppression of crime in Negro neighborhoods. Their actions accentuate the attitude they often express: Negro neighborhoods produce a superabundance of crime, so why should the residents object? When white mothers seek to improve the environment in which their children grow up, they find a more responsive and helpful police department.

Black parents have faced a virtual stone wall as they have tried to improve the educational experience of their children. In spite of heavy taxes, often paid many times over, these parents are in the main unable to bring about improvement in the quality of the education their children receive. White parents have generally found a more responsive Board of Education, and in fact the quality of instruction available to white children in this country is significantly higher than that available to black children.

Black parents are forced to pay fantastic amounts of money for decent housing and are barred by law and custom (restrictive covenants, real estate discrimination condoned by courts) from decent housing at a decent price. And the black parents are absolutely helpless in the face of this collusion among real estate men, landlords, and the courts of law. When a black child notices that a white man with the same job as his father can provide good housing for his family while his father provides him with a slum, that child may draw conclusions about his father's ability to look after his own. But the father may not be incompetent at all; it may simply be that he lives in a smooth-running community where black folk are being contained and are helpless.

The Negro family is in deep trouble. It is coming apart and it is failing to provide the nurturing that black children need. In its failure the resulting isolated men and women fail generally to make a whole life for themselves in a nation designed for families and for white families besides.

A great many of the problems of black people in America can be traced back to the widespread crumbling of the family structure.

But in spite of the many simplistic half-truths that have been uttered, as in Daniel P. Moynihan's celebrated report on the Negro family, the cause of the sickness in black families is not primarily the attack on manhood that discrimination relentlessly carries out. Men have borne that and remained men. It is not urbanization and the demand that the family adjust itself to a new world. Families have done that successfully since the beginning of time. Nor could it be poverty alone, if men were allowed the rights and privileges, the opportunities and assistance which citizens of any nation call their due.

No! No! No! The problem of the Negro family is not these challenges. The problem is a latter-day version of the problem faced by the slave family. How does one build a family, make it strong, and breed from it strong men and women when the institutional structures of the nation make it impossible for the family to serve its primary purpose—the protection of its members?

The Negro family is weak and relatively ineffective because the United States sets its hand against black people and by the strength of wealth, size, and number *prevents* black families from protecting their members.

Moynihan's argument seemed to have been developed in reverse. Starting with the task of providing a sociological basis in theory for a federal program of jobs for Negroes, he was obviously limited to a few concepts which would support his argument.

A program for strengthening black families would have to include a change in the fabric of the nation so that a black man could extend physical protection to his family everywhere, throughout the country. Such a program would include a change in the working of governments so that black people could command that officials serve them, not humiliate them; that policemen protect them, not prey on them. Such a program would see to it that officialdom generally and courts of law in particular occupy themselves with grander matters than keeping black families huddled together in a ghetto for the enrichment of real estate interests.

If to these changes in national life is added a program of jobs for Negroes, then we would agree that substantive aid will have been given the ailing black family.

But in spite of the problems facing them, black couples continue to marry, establish families, and try to make a worthwhile contribution to the stream of life. The husband works as best he can, the wife mothers as best she can, and they love each other as best they can. As they mold their lives together and form a matrix from which children grow, the next most important function of a family, second only to protection and survival, comes into focus: to provide an accurate interpretation of the world to its children. Children must above all be taught what the world is like, how it functions, and how *they* must function if they are to survive and eventually establish their own families. If the family does not convey an accurate image of the world, the children will either succumb or fail to prosper sufficiently to allow them to start their own families. So important is this interpretive function that the natural relationship between children and parents makes it certain that the children will first see the world through the eyes of their parents.

The intimacy, the love, and above all the identification with the parents, not to mention the absence of competing models, all make certain that the child will view the world with the eyes of the parents.

Is it not conceivable that many of the dismal consequences of Negro family life might be related to the world the children first view? The family, we can be certain, has given them an accurate view of the world. If this view is bleak and dismaying, may not the family say to its young:

> It is a terrible place you come to;
> I'm not sure I can hearten you in any way,
> Although I would like to.
> I can only say I have survived—
> I honestly don't know how—
> And you must also survive.

If such a message is indeed conveyed by black families, and surely it must be, then this may account for the fragmenting of the family structure. The family is in fact saying that it has no skills of mastery to pass on, that it has found no way to reliably "make it" in society. It says that one must fight to live; one can only survive, and one *must* survive. This would seem quite enough to shake any young generation.

But families continue to form, to function, and to grow old. The bond which makes it all possible is that between men and women. It is the bedrock, the solace which makes so many darknesses bearable. And even here, in the love relation which makes the family possible, we find the contaminating influence of racial hatred.

A black couple, describing their love-making, said that much of the bantering between them involved invidious comparisons between the wife's sexual desirability and that of any hypothetical white woman. The joking would extend to the idea that white people generally are more attractive, more refined, more natural objects of desire, whereas blacks are deformed, repugnant, and debased. In this polarization of black and white, they would become aroused by the fantasy which made them animal-like and the ensuing sexual experience would be enhanced.

It should be no surprise to find racial issues accompanying a black man to bed. The black man occupies a very special sexual role in American society. He is seen as the ultimate in virility and masculine vigor. But at the same time he is regarded as socially, economically, and politically castrated, and he is gravely handicapped in performing every other masculine role. It is difficult for him to acquire goods for his family, to achieve power in the councils of his fellow men, and, in fact, to fulfill the fundamental role of providing protection for his family. His society has barred him from white women. However much love and passion he feels for his black partner, he cannot help bringing the idea to his bed that only here, and only with her, is he granted the opportunity to function in a truly manly way. Such attitudes carry with them feelings of rage, depression, futility, and, not unexpectedly, sometimes a heighting of sexual excitement. However much he may love his partner, he cannot help seeing, reflected in her, the narrowed range of his own world. She is his black counterpart and is depreciated as much as he. The natural male inclination to obtain and possess a highly valued woman, to compete with other men for her favor, and to win out because of his own strength—none of this does he fulfill with his beloved. He sees her as a depreciated object and this reinforces his own perception of himself as a depreciated man. The enhancement of the sexual act which comes to the male who feels he has laid hold of a prize is absent. Moreover, his depreciation of her and his hostility toward her cannot help being perceived by the woman, and likewise cannot but contribute to her own feeling of degradation.

As mentioned previously, a device may be brought into play which seems an ingenious solution to an otherwise impossible psychological impasse. Because in this society our defenses are set firmly in opposition to sexual impulses, such impulses are experienced as degrading aspects of ourselves and the full drive and power of human sexuality is linked to a feeling of debasement. Thus insofar as the black man sees himself as a cornered, debased, and castrated sexual object, this very perception of himself allows him to circumvent the inhibition of sexual desire. In his degradation he lays hold of a fuller range of sexual powers. It is as if he says: "If I am beast and animal, then let me show you how this animal makes love!"

With this enhancement of his sexual powers his self-esteem rises. Out of his feelings of devaluation come an increase in his feelings as a man and, no doubt, a strengthening of his resolution to enter again into outside competition, that competition which in every other way is so heavily weighted against him.

It is in the nature of women to experience sex as an interplay between narcissism and masochism. As the black woman enters the embrace of her black lover, many of the same ghosts which haunt him now also haunt her, but in a characteristically feminine way. All her life her narcissism has been deeply wounded and impaired. She finds it difficult to experience herself as a highly valued object to whom any man would be drawn. Rather she sees herself as a depreciated, unwanted instrument of no inherent value, to be used by men and society at their pleasure. The bitterness that grows out of such a self-perception augments her already established self-hatred, her feelings of being used, and her feelings of worthlessness.

Under the circumstances she feels hatred and scorn for the man who embraces her, since she sees in him the evidence of her own degradation. Where a woman would otherwise find narcissistic enhancement in being possessed by a powerful lover, she cannot regard the man as either powerful or loving. Instead of narcissistic enhancement, she experiences narcissistic depletion. She hates him for his being castrated in society at large and unable to bring that special increment of power to their loving. She finds herself progressively degraded in the course of the sexual relationship. But again, as happens to her lover, she finds her own erotic feelings strengthened by the feelings of degradation. In the feminine sexual mode these feelings of masochism have a strong erotic component, so that she finds herself not only degraded but masochistically submitting to a man she views as depreciated and participating in an act which furth .epletes her slender narcissistic resources. She finds a sexual reinforcement and strengthening which brings a heightening of erotic pleasure out of the very circumstances which might have initially blunted it.

While this phenomenon of degradation and masochistic submission ultimately serves to strengthen the sexual experience, beyond the world of the black woman it is in large measure a commentary upon the repressive attitudes generally held toward sexual functioning in the Western world. It speaks as much for the adaptability of the human organism as for man's apparently infinite ability to make life difficult for himself.

Sexual union, then, requires a synthesis of real life and fantasy in a way that will make for a vigorous coming together. The fact that their real life is often an oppressed life can impose an additional psychological burden on the black lovers, which serves as a divisive element in the black family and in a significant way contributes to the fragility of that union.

Black men and women have this complex of problems in large measure because they have always been regarded by white Americans as sexual objects, exotic people living close to instinct and primitivism. The fascination black people have for white people in the sexual area can hardly be exaggerated, and this factor alone makes a major contribution to the charged quality of racial relationships in this country.

One result of this sexual tension between the races is a preoccupation with interracial sexual liaisons. The black lover fears that his partner will be tempted by a white seducer. And conversely, his white counterparts feel impotent if challenged by a black rival. One could make a case for mutual lust and jealousy as the basis for racial conflict in America.

But since interracial sexual unions have so infatuated Americans, black and white, and form so large a part of their secret fantasies, some study of these relationships is in order.

When a black man and a white woman unite, one can

assume that unnumbered racially connected issues will arise. For the black man, the white woman represents the *socially identified* female ideal and thus an intensely exciting object for his sexual possession. She has been identified as precisely the individual to whom access is barred by every social institution. The forbiddenness and desirableness of the white woman make her a natural recipient of his projected oedipal fantasies. He sees himself as finally possessing the maternal object under circumstances which reproduce the dangerous, defiant quality of oedipal interest as experienced by the child. He feels a sense of power at having acquired this highly valuable woman and a sense of power that she finds him desirable and indeed that she finds him *more* desirable than a white lover. But at the same time he perceives her as white and as a representative of all the white oppressors who have made his life so wretched. In a sense then, she becomes the target for a hatred which far transcends the encounter between this man and this woman.

The sexual act itself carries aggressive overtones, and in the fantasy of all men there is a likening of male aggression in the sexual act to murderous aggression and a likening of the female partner to the victim of murder. The black man then has an opportunity to live out murderous fantasies of re     e. In possessing the white woman he sees himself as degrading her (a function of his own feelings of degradation), in this instance sharing the community's feeling that a white woman who submits to a black lover becomes as debased as he. In this way he may feel the gratification of turning the tables on his white oppressor and thus becoming the instrument through which a white person is degraded.

Finally, and perhaps most importantly, he sees himself as having vanquished the white man in the field of love and of having rendered him impotent and castrated, for the white woman, in fantasy at least, has embraced a white lover and then chosen a black one. While in every other area of life the black man may feel emasculated and humiliated by the white man, here he can reverse the roles and, because of the central importance of the sexual function in human affairs, may feel that the scales are almost balanced.

His fantasies find reinforcement in the keen delight his partner takes in his embrace. Her delight may rest on her own set of fantasies, but they both know that, whatever the causes may be, she finds more intense gratification from her black lover than she does from her white one.

Should the relationship progress to marriage, the problems increase exponentially, since in this culture marriage progressively downgrades the importance of the sexual act and lays increasing emphasis on the economic and social functioning of the partners. The black man married to a white woman is hounded by the knowledge that outside the bedroom his manhood is compromised. In fact, both the initial delight of his partner and his own intense satisfaction may pall under the certain knowledge that in the outside world he is an emasculated half-man. This places a grave strain on the relationship. The greatest stress seems to come, however, from the perception by the partners of the nature of the world in which they live, a perception which is sufficiently tied to reality to change in response to a change in that external world. The evidence for this is seen in the happy marriages between blacks and whites which flourish outside this country and which emphasize that the love relationship, given half a chance by society, can flourish between people of disparate origins.

The white woman who seeks a black lover finds him to be an intensely exciting sexual partner because of his forbiddenness and because of the ease with which she can project onto him her own oedipal fantasies. Since black people are a minority, representing less than one-tenth of the population, they may not find the physical appearance of the Caucasian so exotic. This is not true for the Caucasian. A white woman finds her black lover sufficiently strange, and she is able to experience the excitement of having a forbidden sexual object as well as a lover who is so different-looking as to allow her to see him as a different kind of human being or even a subhuman animal. She is thus able to experience herself as different or subhuman along with her partner and in that way to participate in sexuality of an intensity and quality forbidden her as "herself," with all of the strictures and inhibitions that go along with that self-perception. Though she may view her black lover as a degraded object, she also views him as a sexual master.

As she submits to him, her own masochistic strivings feed her excitement at ɡ possessed by such a being. These feelings contribute in a major way to her gratification. In his arms she merges with him and abandons her previous identity. In so doing she finds it easy to isolate the experience as a unique, intensely gratifying moment which has no relationship to the rest of her life. The emasculation of her black lover in the outside world makes it easier for her to feel separated and different from him and, in fact, safe from the invasion of her own forbidden fantasies into everyday life.

In fact, her attraction to him may rest in large measure specifically on these grounds. The relationship allows her uninhibited enjoyment of otherwise forbidden sexual impulses without experiencing any threat to her life generally. Should such a union eventuate in marriage, she would likely be concerned primarily with his ability to bring home the bacon, and if she found him lacking in this respect, her resulting bitterness might well cause her latent hostility toward all black people to emerge.

If, on the other hand, she experienced no disadvantages economically, her primary concern would surely focus on the social problems they met as a couple. The contempt she would encounter from the majority of white people would be a constant burden and the contempt she would feel when they saw her with her brown children would cause even greater pain.

A white woman had enjoyed a happy marrige to a black man for six years. During this time she rarely saw her mother. But when her mother became seriously ill, she sat by her bedside and promised God that if her mother survived she would never again cause her pain.

Her mother recovered and the patient developed severe anxiety, phobias, and in fact a pan-neurosis. She became hypersensitive to the stares of white people when she appeared in public with her brown children. She refused to go out in public with her husband and discouraged physical intimacy. At the same time she sought to reestablish a close relationship with her mother.

What had been to all appearances a happy marriage dissolved as this woman required a great sacrifice of herself. She had to undo the greatest pain she had caused her mother, marriage to a black man.

The white woman who is married to a black man feels her most intense discomfort in the relationship when she considers her children, the contempt in which they may be held, and the difficulties they may encounter as a result of mixed parentage. Her misery will subside only when they are married and she no longer suffers with them for every rebuff they receive.

The relationship which has the longest history and the most complex psychological structure is the relationship between the white man and the black woman. From the very first introduction of black slaves into America, black women have been used sexually by their white owners. In contrast to the male slaves they had a threefold use—their labor was economically valuable, their bodies had a marketable value as sexual objects, and their potential as breeders of additional slaves was also a source of wealth to their owners.

Even now in many areas a black woman has no protection from the sexual appetites of white men. In the raw circumstance of power and the imposition of the will of the powerful on the weak, the most significant aspect of the woman's position is her helplessness against sexual assault. She cannot protect herself against sexual use by a powerful male. Her only protection lies in binding herself sexually to a powerful man who can in turn protect her from other men. It would seem that both the erotic component of a woman's masochism and her tendency to gain narcissistic gratification from being chosen by a powerful man make it easy for her to yield herself to a powerful man and to gain special gratification out of such submission. In addition, a woman need feel no qualms of conscience if she is taken sexually against her will and must submit to the sexual act under pain of violence. Under such circumstances her own conscience, moral code, and inhibitions stand in suspension.

All these factors are important in the manner in which a black woman relates herself to a white lover. However weak in fact he may be, however ineffective and poor, he is potentially more powerful than any black lover. He is a part of and a representative of the powerful white majority—a representative of the wealth and prestige accrued in the United States and throughout the Western world over the past two thousand years.

In a historical sense, she, on the other hand, stands in the position of all the black people who have been exploited and dominated by white men since the beginning of recorded time. In a historical sense and in a very real contemporary sense, she faces a powerful lover. The prospect of sexually submitting to him evokes excitement in her. In addition to the explicit pleasure involved in masochistic submission, she gains some of the strength and power of the white man.

An attractive black wife and mother sought out a highly recommended white professional man and in his consultation room began describing in a very businesslike manner the relevant issues which had brought her to his office. After listening to her briefly he got up from his desk, came around, kissed her, took off her clothes, and made love to her. He then told her he would look after her problems and dismissed her.

What is of special interest here is the frame of mind of the woman during the episode in the white professional's office. In treatment later she recounted that she had been chaste as a single woman and faithful as a wife but found herself strangely submissive and yielding to this man. In fact she was intensely aroused by the experience. Her associations were of his impressive office, his wide reputation, his apparent wealth and power. While there were other determinants to her behavior, the relation of her passivity to his power and the aggressive manner in which he thrust himself on her are instructive.

This type of passive submission, strongly colored by eroticism, has historically characterized the relationship between black women and white men. It is the converse of the relationship between black men and white women. The black man is highly excited by possessing the valuable ideal female and the black woman is intensely aroused at being subdued and possessed by the powerful white man. His power, desirability, and forbiddenness evoke her own oedipal fantasies and she finds herself particularly gratified that this powerful man chooses her in preference to a white woman.

In her relationship with a white man, the black woman can partake of his power and masculinity and can for once free herself of her degraded self-perception. In his embrace she is whole again and can experience the sexual act as simply a woman submitting to a desirable man. Her own thwarted narcissistic strivings can for once find embodiment in a lover whose possibilities for living them out are apparently limitless—an experience she cannot have with a black lover.

To the extent that she sees her own blackness as ugly and repellent, her possession of a white lover and her identification with him allow her to view herself as white and therefore beautiful. The problem arises, however, when she must leave his bed and face the real world again. However much her white lover protests his devotion to her, she is beset with feelings of self-depreciation, depression, and futility. She sees herself as having been used and debased for the satisfaction of a powerful man who only took advantage of her weakness and susceptibility. She perceives herself as having striven for something beyond her, and her remorse is her "punishment" for "reaching above her station." Should she return to a black lover, she might well feel herself all the more degraded and oppressed.

If her relationship with the white man leads to marriage, the prospect is that as the bloom of romance fades she will find herself dreading that he will abandon her. Past experiences make her feel truly worthless and undesirable. It is only in his arms that she feels a whole woman, sexually desirable to men. Away from him she is again potentially the ugly, despised black woman. She is convinced that he has a false perception of her which makes her seem beautiful and desirable to him, and she dreads the moment when he sees her as she sees herself and, in revulsion, thrusts her away from him. Her position is a wretched one.

On the other side of the coin, the white man, by taking to himself a black woman, acts in defiance of all socially accepted norms. Our society allows a white man to surreptitiously experiment with black women sexually but never to take one into a love relationship. As a prostitute or as a casual mistress, a black woman can be a meaningless sexual toy and involvement with her need have no profound effect on his life. Psychologically, he can look upon her as a debased human animal who finds pleasure in a sexual life no decent woman would tolerate. The uninhibited pleasures he shares with her might serve to further dichotomize his emotional life, and his relationship with his white wife might suffer. But beyond this there need be no grave disruption of his functioning.

If, on the other hand, the black woman assumes some emotional importance for him, his problems are compounded. It is likely that he would enter into a relationship only in response to feelings of defiance toward the social order generally, and perhaps his family or parents specifically. Under these circumstances the black woman serves a *specific* psychological purpose for him because of her general unacceptability as a mate.

Whatever gratification the two of them might share in their union, her role as evidence of his defiance and her functioning as a social curiosity will clearly limit the richness of their relationship and dull their satisfaction. In any event, in the United States, the psychological truth is that when a white man chooses a black woman, both in his own eyes and in the eyes of his confreres, he has chosen a depreciated sexual object rather than a highly valued one. This factor is obviously of greater social importance than the desirability of the black woman as an exotic and forbidden representative of his inner desires. Such fantasies and strivings allow him to act out unconscious wishes which intensify his pleasure. The social value set on each of the partners reverses their roles, making him the highly valued object whom the woman has been fortunate enough to obtain.

His own narcissism is enhanced thereby and he finds a special gratification in their relationship. He feels constantly inferior to black men, however, feeling that sexually he is less satisfying as a partner than *any* black man. He is the victim of the stereotype which played such an important part in his choosing a black woman in the first place.

If their relationship develops into marriage, his fantasies inevitably lead him into doubts about his wife's fidelity. It is easy for him to become dissatisfied with her and feel the lack of a *desirable* woman whose *desirability* would enhance his own self-esteem. His role as the more desirable of the pair fades in importance.

Again, the evidence is clear that however much misery the black woman and white man experience in their relationship, their suffering is remarkably alleviated by living in a community which does not contain the intense social hostility of communities in the United States. If they moved to Europe or Latin America, they would have a better chance of operating in terms of their individual compatibility, much as any other couple, and of finding fulfillment in their union without special reference to their racial difference. The factor which militates heavily against such unions is the society rather than the racial origins of the pair.

However troubled his mating and however fragile his union with his woman, the black man has found sufficient nourishment to endure and bring forth issue, to exploit his strengths, and to relentlessly attack the social order which limits the expanse of this most precious place.

# ░ VI ░

## *Character Traits*

Traits of character and patterns of behavior that appear more often in black people than in other groups can all be traced to various aspects of life in America. Cultural anthropologists have searched intensively and interminably and have found no contemporary evidence for the persistence of African patterns of culture. The experience of slavery was unbelievably efficient in effacing the African and producing the American Negro. As a result, the cultural and characterological patterns developed by American Negroes provide a unique picture of a people whose history was destroyed and who were offered in its stead a narrow ledge of toil on which to live and grow and nurture children. All that is uniquely Negro found its origin on these shores and provides a living document of black history in America.

I

The interaction among members in black families is increasingly responding to many of the pressures which shape life in other ethnic groups in America. The superficial aspects are the most readily affected, in part because deeper themes and roles are more resistant to change and because the instruments of change are aimed precisely at the superficial aspects of life. But beneath the apparent similarities there run consistent threads—ways of life shared by most black people.

The black family is first of all an extended family. Relatives more readily share the responsibilities of child-rearing. Members of the family more often come to the aid of a troubled member.

In a child-guidance clinic which served a large number of black children, it was found easy to take a black child out of an explosive home situation and lodge him temporarily with a relative in the South. This generally produced good long-term results. Among whites, relatives *and the immediate family* were more resistant to such solutions.

When a brother is asked where *home* is, he is likely to answer promptly: "Montgomery, Alabama," even if he has lived in Cleveland, Ohio, for the past forty-seven years. Home is where the land was and where "one's people" are. The answer might be further refined with the explanation: "Montgomery is my home but all my *people* are in Birmingham." Where my people are is part of my essential self and where I first dug my fingers in soil is a vital part of me. Geography is thus part of the extended identity as is the extended family.

It has a further implication. Away from one's home and people, one is merely a sojourner. However long one lives away from home, the roots reach back to one's people. Cleveland may represent merely a forty-seven-year visit away from home. When death comes, the body is taken home. Thus our brother is never in a true sense a Clevelander. However much his community makes him feel an outsider, he himself provides an additional increment of alienation. As a protective device, he says it was never his city anyway.

The viciousness of life in America for black men makes them remove themselves even further. If I establish first that I am a stranger in your land, I will at least avoid the shock of being attacked in my own home by kinfolk. We are strangers and I dwell for a while in your world—therefore, whatever you do to me cannot truly come as a surprise.

In this world of strangers black men make a home wherever they can. Any black man in a white environment can establish a relationship with another black man by a glance or an easy salutation such as "Hey, bro"—and he has a colleague.

In years gone by a most delightful relationship existed between porters and waiters on passenger trains and the infrequent black traveler. A man could put his child on the train, press a dollar into the hand of the porter, and ask him to "look after her"—and he could rest easy. It was a source of pride for train employees to lavish care and affection on their brethren. The charm of a dining-car waiter in caring for a frightened black girl would have to be seen to be appreciated. It was as if these men were thumbing their noses at the railroad company as they provided million-dollar service to impoverished black travelers. This small body of true aristocrats has lately fallen on hard times, but some future complex of services will no doubt find dark men extending a special hand of welcome to dark brothers.

More than any other place, however, the barbershop is the black man's way station, point of contact, and universal home. Here he always finds a welcome—a friendly audience as he tells his story and a native to give him the word on local doings.

The bickering, the sniping, the backbiting so often said to characterize black people in their relationship with one another seems so very much to be the rivalry of siblings. Underlying it all is a feeling that "you're no better than I." It is an unfortunate corollary of such a feeling of "sibship," but it is probably a small price to pay for the comfort and the web of support provided by a brotherhood.

The family is broad; the self has roots in many places. The brother has several selves and many homes. A creature of prey must have more than one haven.

"It's a poor rat that don't have but one hole."


# II

A black mechanic who had a good income as owner of his own repair shop dissipated his profits and when pressed by creditors ran crap games in his place of business to raise money. Reminded that he had a major investment in his business which was jeopardized by the gambling, he threw up his hands and said: "I'll never make nothing no way."

He was an excellent mechanic and had demonstrated above-average ability from his earliest years. He was raised in the South and at the age of ten was maintaining complicated machinery. With little formal schooling he nevertheless became skillful at various machine operations. He had developed a potentially thriving business single-handedly. But what he later described so eloquently was his lack of faith in that which he accomplished with his own hands. The ownership of property had been a source of misery for his father. White rivals, with the collusion of southern courts, had overnight taken the fruits of years of labor. He himself as a young man had been swindled by white men. The crucial factor here is that he had no recourse. The courts, the state, the citizenry—all were poised to accuse *him* if he objected to being robbed.

In his behavior he seemed to be saying that he could not hope to accumulate goods from his own labor. They could be taken away so swiftly that it was better not even to consider them his own. The more he owned, the more anxious he became. He turned then to luck; if fortune smiled he was saved. Otherwise he faced bankruptcy.

A man cannot develop an intense emotional invest-ment in land if it can be taken away at any moment. The interlocking of business interests in any community, particularly in the South, can effectively prevent a black man from accumulating goods by denying him funds and supplies and, in general, blocking his access to commerce. If by some chance he does acquire land or goods, they can be taken away by the same association of business interests in his community. The reader who is skeptical probably bases his doubts on his own experience, but black people have been robbed of their goods as well as their labor throughout their sojourn in this country.

In the 1950's a young white southern lawyer, newly returned from a New England law school, was assigned a case by his law firm involving a Negro woman and her property. He soon realized that his task was to have the woman committed to an institution as insane and to arrange for the acquisition of her property by a client of the law firm. He resigned from the firm and took on the woman's defense. He learned of similar cases and, by defending them, earned the enmity of his colleagues. Threats were made on his life and he fled the state for his own safety.

The brother with property in the South is highly visible and is usually the target for business rivals. What would otherwise be healthy competition becomes under these circumstances a deadly game of defense in which the most he can hope for is to avoid capture. Retaliation is out of the question.

Thus for black people the ability to divorce oneself emotionally from an object is necessary for survival.

The mechanic's response is neurotic but the surrounding reality fosters his symptom. Does anyone know of a community where a small businessman who happens to be black does not face greater problems of survival than his white confreres? And if such is the case, does not his fate really lie with chance rather than his own effort?

To label this response improvident, to call the man naive or inexperienced in the ways of business, is to close one's eyes to the nature of the society in which he lives. It is a refusal to recognize the social soil in which his attitudes grow.

The journals of slaveowners tell of their exasperation when their slaves refused to work or worked poorly or broke farm tools. They attributed such behavior to "poor moral fiber," shiftlessness, and stupidity. One wonders who is stupid, the slave who dawdles or the owner who expected him to do otherwise.

And one wonders how long a man can maintain enthusiasm for thrift, diligence, and hard work when the rewards so earned are denied and when the goods so earned are stolen.

We suggest that there is no more subtle student of American society than the black man, and when he suspects that he is called to a race where there is no prize, he simply declines to run.

One additional word on the matter of property. The land to which Africans were brought and which their labor made great was simply an outpost in the wilds of North America when they first were pressed into bondage. Their labor produced tobacco, the first significant agricultural product to supplement the precarious shipping industry. When in the early 1800's the European demand for cotton made it a prime cash crop, blacks were imported in huge numbers. When cotton became king, it rested solely on black backs. Cotton, or the slaves who produced it, moved this nation from a colonial outpost in 1800 to an industrial giant of the twentieth century. The labor of blacks and its product were the bridge and, importantly, the only bridge from world insignificance to world dominance in slightly more than a century. As certain as is history—America is the wealthiest nation in the world because of the labor of black men.

One further item: when a slaveowner found his land exhausted from too intense cultivation of cotton, he sold the slaves to purchase machinery and fertilizer which would allow him to diversify his crops. From this point of view, blacks occupied a central place in the nation's economy.

The Civil War came at a time when cotton no longer held its pre-eminent position and when industrialization was on the rise. The time had passed when the labor of black slaves made such an overriding difference to the economy of the country. Their labor in the fields would be important for another sixty years, but by 1865 the future of the country was secure and the cynic may be excused if he notes that the national repugnance for slavery developed only at a time when its loss did the nation little harm.

Since 1865 the most significant economic development for blacks has been the systematic theft of the lands acquired by this agricultural people. The labor required for an ex-slave to lay hold of an eighty-acre plot of land was prodigious, but the speed with which he could be robbed of it was dizzying.

Quite aside from the moral issue, the historical picture makes America's treatment of blacks somewhat more comprehensible. They were brought here to be exploited and that exploitation has continued to this very date. Robbed of lands, they were denied worthwhile employment in the growing industrial complex. They were drafted into the labor force in times of stress and need, such as war, as easily as they were drafted into military service. When the emergency was past, they were dismissed. They were swept into commercial enterprises as laborers when they could be used tactically—as, for example, by the growing auto industry to spike the guns of organized labor or indeed by organized labor to undo the automakers. In all these involvements they were pawns—kept poor, uneducated, and powerless.

Now the purpose of this shuttlecock game in which the brother is the cock was not lost on dark men. They and their labor have always been used for the enrichment of white men. And as the idea of private property is so important in American society and acquisitiveness has become a virtue, it is not surprising that black people have on occasion developed a uniquely flexible concept of ownership.

Men reduced to the status of non-persons and removed from the protection of the social code can hardly be expected to honor the responsibilities imposed by that code. And men (now emancipated) excluded from all benefit of the social order, indeed preyed upon by that social order, may wear lightly the injunction that (a white man's) property is sacred. No, we grant that it is likely that blacks steal more than whites, but we suggest that there is no more efficient way to produce a thief than to steal a man's substance and command that he hold his peace.

## III

We take the position that there is a grain of truth in every stereotypical canard tossed at the brothers. But we move a step further. A close examination of the trait, its psychological roots, and its predictable transformations may yield interesting conclusions. Oppression which is capable of producing paralyzing fear and paranoia may under slightly different circumstances produce the deadliest of enemies. Black people are sometimes said to be easily frightened, easily intimidated, and readily persuaded by a show of force. Consider an alternative reaction in the following case:

A young sergeant obtained his discharge from the military after ten years of service and three years of combat. He returned to his home, a small southern town, to visit with his family before looking for permanent employment. He drank too much in a bar one night and fell asleep on the bus. When he awakened he was in a strange neighborhood. He jumped off the bus and asked a white man where he was. The man screamed for help and a nearby neighbor ran out with a gun. The police were summoned and the sergeant was accused of attempted robbery. He was convicted and sentenced to three years in prison. The segregated prison was a hell hole. He engaged in bloody battles to defend himself against homosexual assault. He took refuge in reading the Bible and taught some of the other prisoners to read. In spite of the opposition of prison authorities, he developed a modest educational program for the other inmates. When released he wandered about the country doing odd jobs, neglected his appearance, and was jailed from time to time for vagrancy. He asked a friend to call one of the authors for an appointment and duly presented himself in rags and tatters. He said he had no money but he would work twenty hours a day if only someone could help him. He said that while in that southern prison some white man had done something to his mind—could he please be hypnotized so the cause could be found? He knew that something was wrong with his mind because he heard voices now and could not concentrate. He asked: Was there help for him?

Clinically, at that point he was a severe chronic paranoid schizophrenic. This remarkable story was substantiated on all major counts from outside sources.

Imagine the sustained pressure required to induce or trigger a schizophrenic response in a vigorous young man who had functioned successfully as a soldier for ten years and had been in combat for three. This pressure must have offered him no chance of escape or even the hope of a chance. Even years later, sick through and through, there was yet vigor and drive in his determination to get well. Consider for a moment what an enemy the white men *almost* had—a seasoned, resourceful, highly trained killer.

In another season his like may not go mad.

If blacks are often frightened, consider what frightens them and consider what happens when they feel cornered, when there is no further lie one can believe, when one finally sees that he is permanently cast as the victim, and when finally the sleeping giant wakes and turns upon his tormentors.

# IV

A brother died and went to heaven. He was appropriately outfitted with white robe, halo, and wings. The wings fascinated him; he fluttered them, stretched them, and began tentatively to fly. As he gained experience he tried long swooping glides, he flew high, he flew low, he flew backward, he flew upside down, and finally he made dive-bombing attacks on the peaceful citizenry below. Swoosh—within inches of the golden streets. Down over their heads he came, scaring the hell out of cherubim and seraphim. Finally his antics were too much for the management to bear and he was grounded, his wings removed and locked up. As he sat forlornly on the curb a black brother came up.

"Now ain't you a bitch—the way you were performing and carrying on. I told you you were going to lose your wings. If you'd listened to me you'd still have them. No, you had to perform—and now here you sit grounded with no wings!"

The miscreant looked up. "But I was a flying son of a bitch while I had 'em, wasn't I!"

This is the humor of the ghetto and there is no denying it: the brother has a streak of hedonism and a capacity for joy. He drinks more, dances more, and loves more. All suffering people turn in their sorrow to laugh at themselves; they laugh to keep from crying.

An enthusiastic embrace of joyful things is eminently adaptive, indeed necessary to allow the black man to pursue the watchful, careful threading of his way through the hazards of daily life in America.

## V

The subtle, adaptive quality of some character traits may seem apparent but are all the more wonderful when examined in detail. The consultation room provides an excellent setting for such study and the clinical examination of a bit of behavior offers an excitement of its own.

Some years ago an impressive black man of seasoned years sought consultation regarding a relative. He was seen for several lengthy discussions. With little formal education he had established a service business which was thriving and he had shown himself adept, indeed gifted, in quickly learning the principles of business management. He was thoughtful and perceptive about a wide range of subjects. He seemed to look about him with clear eyes and shrewdly assess the world in which he lived—usually with an eye to his own advantage. It was striking, therefore, to hear his speech. He used "dis," "dat," "ain't," "y'all," "bofe," in a manner recalling the radio serial of "Amos 'n' Andy." It seemed extraordinary that this man who showed such a grasp of the appropriate style of dress, complex business practices, and the subtleties of life in the big city should cling to a manner of speech of his childhood in the South. Since it was apparently not to his advantage in advancing his business fortunes, the question remained: Why did he not adapt to the speech of those around him as he had their general style of living?

Sometime later a patient who presented a similar puzzle gave us an opportunity for more detailed study of this phenomenon.

An examination of the psychiatric literature shows the material on speech to be grouped under three primary headings. A great many articles have to do with speech disorders or peculiarities which are specific manifestations of neurotic conflict. Such difficulties may be related to the utterance of certain phrases or unaccountable shifts in quality or timbre of speech. There have also been reported sudden reversions to the language of youth but this was temporary and represented the transient expression of conflict. Another sizable body of literature addresses itself to the precipitates in speech patterns of early oral experiences. Here the emphasis has been on tracing back through speech patterns in order to link up or uncover early determinants of current behavior or character structure. Finally, there is a considerable body of material on specific speech disorders such as stuttering or lisping. Here again the emphasis has been on the speech disorder as a symptom having its roots in one or more conflicts and generally expressing the forbidden impulse on the one hand and the inhibition on the other.

While all these studies on special aspects of the problem are germane to our discussion and to some extent offer new insights, none seems to highlight the peculiar range and strength of the determinants of this phenomenon and certainly none explores the subtle relationship between speech, identity, and blackness in the United States.

Booker is a thirty-five-year-old black man of heroic physical proportions. An athlete in his youth, he maintained an active interest and involvement in sports and his muscular development showed it clearly. He wore his hair very short, almost shaved, and the total effect was of power and strength. He came to treatment because of the sudden onset of anxiety attacks associated with a series of disagreements with his wife which resulted in a separation. He was depressed. His work had begun to suffer. He was an uninhibited gambler and his financial affairs were a shambles. At the outset he said that, unless therapy could help him, all was lost, and though he doubted its efficacy, he engaged himself actively in treatment. His anxiety subsided and he tried to bring his life back into order.

His speech was the patois of the rural uneducated southern Negro of seventy-five years ago. He spoke slowly at times, made an effort to use the proper verb and tense, but it was a great effort for him to speak more properly. He seemed to revert with relief and pleasure to the idiom.

The therapist learned that he had not only been born in a large northern city but had completed his schooling there, obtained an undergraduate and a graduate degree at a major university, and was presently enrolled at the university in a doctoral program. One can only imagine the therapist's astonishment when he revealed that his degree was to be obtained in Speech! His instructors had warned him that he had to do some work on his speech patterns, and he was struggling with this problem.

The therapist frankly found this hard to believe, but it was true that he was enrolled as he said. It was possible, though, that he might have one manner of speech for the consultation room and another for the classroom. Careful questioning, however, established that this was not so. We are then left with the situation of a man who speaks the most idiomatic patois of southern Negroes, who has had extensive educational and vocational exposure to people who speak in a more conventional manner, who is now embarked on a doctoral program in Speech (the dynamic implications of this will be dealt with later), and who maintains this manner of speech despite the serious personal disadvantage to which it subjects him.

We turn to his personal history for enlightenment. Booker was the older of two children born to a young, high-spirited couple. The mother had been a chorus girl and the father a professional gambler. Their union was not legalized and after a few years the father drifted away, leaving the mother to support the children. The maternal grandmother lived with the small family and looked after the children while the mother worked. The father took only a desultory interest in the children; he gave expensive gifts at Christmas but refused to provide regular support. Booker's memories are particularly vivid. His father prospered and bought expensive cars and clothes. Booker remembers his father as always in good humor, always telling some clever trick he had played on a victim.

The father married a young, attractive woman, and Booker recalls seeing them sweep away in big cars. To this day the father seems to be doing well. He is now retired from active business, looks after his property, and takes long vacations—still in good humor—still telling how he tricks the foolish. He remains parsimonious in his dealings with Booker, however. He has no recollection of the father coming to his aid when he needed him, even though the older man had ample resources.

The mother worked hard for many years and during this period had liaisons with several men. Her involvements kept her removed from Booker and his younger brother. She is recalled as an attractive, warm woman who was always busy. Booker tried to blame first his father, then his mother, for his own unhappiness as a child, but he arrived only at a vague neutral attitude in which the father "did what he had to do" and the mother "worked very hard." Specific memories and attitudes were related to the father, but little that was meaningful was recalled about the mother. His warm, intimate experiences were associated with his grandmother. She was the one who baked special dishes for him. She saved to give him a special gift at Christmas, and she was the one for whom he planned special gifts on Mother's Day.

In summary, his childhood was spent in deepest poverty. The family rarely had enough clothing, often was insufficiently fed, and was always poorly housed. Booker shined shoes, washed cars, sold newspapers, and all his efforts were needed to augment the family income. A bright, capable student, he did well up to high school. At that point his athletic abilities were recognized and he was encouraged to complete high school and go to college. His college years were interrupted by military service, during which he got married. He said that he had always been ambitious and he had attended the university up to the time he entered treatment.

In the course of treatment it became clear that Booker was an extremely adept seducer. He seemed particularly to pride himself on his ability to spot a girl in the course of his day, make her acquaintance, and go to bed with her that very night. These involvements contributed to his marital difficulty, but he continued them nonetheless. He spoke at some length regarding his technique, and he stressed the effectiveness of his voice and his patois upon women. He felt that the secret of his success lay in his ability to flatter convincingly *within* the patois, and he believed that this worked whatever the race or cultural background of the woman. His affairs cut across all racial and cultural lines. As he described his technique, it became clear that he was simply a gifted seducer. This raised several questions: Why did he attribute his success to his speech when his broader range of capabilities explained the matter so much more thoroughly? What is the curious position occupied by his speech? In his conception of himself, why does he promote it to a central position here but ignore the consequences in his work and academic efforts?

This case history of one man may help us understand the broader phenomenon of the persistence of maladaptive speech patterns in black Americans. In our view, speech patterns, or accents, announce to the world an essential quality of the speaker's identity. He is telling all who will listen who he is, and stating that this aspect of his identity forms an essential element of his character structure.

An examination of Booker's childhood will make clear his need for solid masculine figures to incorporate and build on in the fashioning of his own masculine identity. His father seemed eminently capable of dealing with a world which must have seemed puzzling and overwhelming to the boy. No doubt Booker's unwillingness to express his hostility in response to his father's rejection is explained by his need to retain the father in a psychological relationship to himself for purposes of incorporation and identification. The father's minimal education and disinterest in education may have contributed to his speech patterns. But no doubt there were inner reasons of his own, perhaps not unlike Booker's, which caused him to cling to this manner of speech.

Booker recognized the significance of his father's speech only in treatment, when he recalled that over the telephone he was often mistaken for his father. He felt a warm glow when he was told this. He came to recognize that in one sense he was displaying his father's banner in his speech, saying in effect that, no matter what the price, it is important to me to be my father's son—to partake of his manners and bind his strengths to me as my own.

Only now does one begin to sense the psychological currents which allow this man to flaunt the most outrageous patois in the face of Ph.D. committees.

If we may make another excursion, we might ponder some implications in several scenes from Shakespeare. In *Henry V,* Harry, in courting Katharine, says:

> Fair Katharine, and most fair,
> Will you vouchsafe to teach a soldier terms
> Such as will enter at a lady's ear
> And plead his love-suit to her gentle heart?

And later adds that he

> Cannot look greenly, nor gasp out my eloquence.

He offers himself as a rough soldier skilled only in the arts of war and asks that she accept him thus.

This is the same king who has only recently given the most stirring exhortation to his troops—a battle call that ranks as a high point in English literature—and from the lips of Shakespeare's greatest warrior king at the zenith of his career.

Othello is the commanding general of the greatest commercial power of the sixteenth century. His military feats are legendary, and Shakespeare gives him some of the most heroic lines and some of the sweetest lines in all literature. As he describes his wooing of Desdemona, he says:

> . . . I spoke of most disastrous chances,
> Of moving accidents by flood and field,
> Of hair-breadth scapes i' th' imminent deadly breach,
> Of being taken by the insolent foe
> And sold to slavery, of my redemption thence
> And portance in my travel's history . . .

> . . . These to hear
> Would Desdemona seriously incline;
> But still the house-affairs would draw her thence,
> Which ever as she could with haste dispatch,
> She'd come again, and with a greedy ear
> Devour up my discourse . . .

Here Othello freely admits his magical and hypnotic way with words. And yet he had said only a few moments previously:

> . . . Rude am I in my speech,
> And little bless'd with the soft phrase of peace

Othello presents himself as a man of crude speech, called upon to woo his bride in the highly sophisticated world of Venice and to defend himself before the most subtle judges in the Western world.

This device, dear to Shakespeare, of having powerful, articulate men presenting themselves in sophisticated environs as stumbling, unschooled boys—this device, when coupled with their soaring words and triumphant acts, is a sure dramatic touch and conveys the supreme confidence of the warrior-lover, whose impassioned speech is infinitely more eloquent than the archaic discourse of courts.

But what have we to learn from two Shakespearean characters, an adept seducer and a shrewd businessman, regarding a function of speech among black people?

Let us begin our examination with an eye to history. When African slaves were brought to this country, they were selected and grouped so that each would have come from a different tribe. In this way the slaveowners sought to avoid communication between the slaves and prevent conspiracy. In addition, it was forbidden to teach slaves to read and write. They were to learn only the practical language of the field, and that from the lips of their masters and overseers. As a result, the slaves learned English as a series of garbled, half-understood, mispronounced words shared mainly by the few slaves on the same plantation. The psychological importance of this device should not be underestimated, for the slaves were even *taught to speak* by their masters.

However, the slaves turned the language as it was presented to them to their own purposes, and in fact to the precise purposes which their owners sought to prevent. While their mispronunciations and misunderstandings were a source of great amusement to the owners, the garbled patois began to be used as a secret language among the slaves. Language was used with a particular emphasis on double meanings. In fact, multiple meanings were imposed on language. as, for example, in the spirituals. To the uninformed listener the words spoke of religious longing; the singing provided a harmonious accompaniment to their work, and to the viewer all was piety and submission. The true meaning of the spirituals, however, involves a communication from one to another regarding plans for escape, hostile feelings toward the master, and a general expression of rebellious attitudes. As the language of any group provides a feeling of identity and group unity, the patois of the slaves came to take on a meaning and purpose for them. But all the while no slave could deny that his speech remained a badge of inferiority in the eyes of the whites. The slaves had turned this badge to their own devices as best they could.

Out of the interaction between slave and master and the isolated nature of southern living, the southern dialect as used by whites in the South also came to reflect certain aspects of the slave culture. The southern dialect is a slow, leisurely, gracious, often devious meandering around an idea which has a scholarly, patient, highly civilized quality about it. At its best, it reflects a way of life involving man's highest aspirations, a passionate devotion to honesty, humility, learning, compassion. At its worst, it has a brutal, primitive quality that is shocking to other English-speaking peoples. It is in the latter light that the realities of the slave culture are reflected in the language. In fact, the polarization of attitudes reflected in the language expresses the intense ambivalence of life in the southern United States. The tentative, tendentious quality of the language is often used to obscure the inconsistencies in the life of the Southerner. Things which cannot be faced squarely are covered over with an obscuring scrim of softening words.

In the later years of slavery, when some slaves were able to master the language, and after the emancipation of slaves from bondage, a proliferation of schools enabled large numbers of ex-slaves to learn the language, but still the indirectness of southern language patterns fitted the needs of the oppressed black minority perfectly. In the circumlocution so necessary to the beleaguered blacks it became a more refined art.

In contemporary Negro life the patois of old is ubiquitous. Those few highly refined black people who say they cannot speak the patois do not deny that they understand it thoroughly when spoken by someone else. It remains essentially the language a black man uses with his fellows and continues to represent past years of bondage. In this sense it is despised and rejected by many Negroes. Thus we can see how the patois has served a wide-ranging adaptive function for black people from the earliest days of enslavement in the United States down to the present.

If we are willing to agree that the primary adaptive purpose of the patois during slavery is no longer functional —that is, conspiracies and escapes are no longer discussed in words of double meaning—and if also it is clear that the patois now brands its user with a great many negative attributes, and if further we appreciate the ease with which a more generally acceptable manner of speech can be acquired, we must then look for other explanations for the continuation of the patois in general usage among blacks. Explanations are likely to be found in the unconscious usages to which such speech is put.

In this sense one important unconscious use of the patois rests on the Negro's perception, and, in fact, his white confrere's perception as well, that the true status of the races in the United States at this time is that Negroes are regarded as slaves who are no longer officially enslaved. In this light the same attitudes exist on the part of the white majority toward the black minority and the hostility and aggression which the white potentially feels toward the black must be dealt with by Negroes who seek to live in this country. The patois, then, may continue to serve the purpose it served originally during the period of enslavement. Out of fear and out of the brutal necessity of dealing with a white oppressor, the black American must from time to time convey to the white person that he is aware that he is perceived as inferior—and is at least nominally willing to agree that he is inferior. Thus the patois continues to serve an adaptive function even though the circumstances to which adaptation must be made are less clear-cut and the nature of the adaptation itself may be unconscious.

Still driven to this verbal depreciation, the black man puts the patois again to his own uses. The "jive" language and the "hip" language, while presented in a way that whites look upon simply as a quaint ethnic peculiarity, is used as a secret language to communicate the hostility of blacks for whites, and great delight is taken by blacks when whites are confounded by the language.

One step removed is the music of Negroes. Black musicians have always sought to express something uniquely black and to express it in a way which leaves whites dumfounded and excluded. Most popular music in America expresses this progressive change in the manner of expression of black musicians. No sooner have some whites learned the special techniques than Negro musicians develop a new, more difficult technique, and when that too can be shared by whites, another more complex idiom is developed. Any student of contemporary music can follow this evolution and will be impressed by the technical and theoretical developments black musicians have moved toward in response to the drive for a unique and ethnically singular method of expression.

Blacks today continue to follow the patterns of slavery times. By appearing to accept the ethnic stereotypes that are intended to depreciate them, they turn these stereotypes to their own group purpose. The idea that Negroes have natural rhythm was originally used by whites to depreciate any musical creativity observed among blacks. Today this stereotype is embraced by black people and elaborated in the creation of a singular music which the white cannot create and which he can neither play nor understand. In the concept of "soul," black people agree that they can sing and dance and experience music in a way that whites cannot. The stereotype that Negroes have some kind of animal-like capacity to excel in athletic events is embraced by blacks who say: "Yes, we are stronger, swifter, and more beautifully coordinated than the whites."

And as for the stereotype of the black man's sexual superiority, which has many psychological roots but is offered in a depreciating way as evidence of his more animal-like and less civilized nature, to this black people add an emphatic "Yes!"

Thus the patois and the other demeaning attributes are turned to a positive and elevating use, and continue to bind black people together with a sense of identity and group solidarity.

And in a manner that is characteristic of the unconscious, the patois which was imposed as a brand of humiliation, defeat, and suffering, and which by force of circumstance had to be incorporated and made a part of black people in the United States, has been turned to express defiance against the oppressor and, in a subtle but significant way, vanquishment of the white oppressor. The vanquishment can be seen in the following:

> A group of black men were asked to describe their techniques of seduction. Without exception each said that at a crucial point he reverted to the patois. Black women said that they experienced an intensification of excitement when their lovers reverted to the "old language."

It is as if in his sexual conquests the black man welcomes the opportunity to show his skill, his desirability, and his superiority over his white oppressor in the ultimate competition men engage in.

In a more important sense then, the black businessman whom we introduced earlier understood his environment better than his interviewer. In the competition of the business world it was no doubt of great use to him to ingratiate himself with white men through the manner of his speech and in this way soften their view of him. His speech patterns no doubt had many other determinants, but it is clear that he persisted in this pattern of speech mainly because of the nature of the business environment in which he operated. His speech served to soften the hostility of competition. The case history of Booker emphasizes the more defiant and challenging quality of clinging to such speech patterns. Booker must have been most persuasive and determined to convince the university that he should be accepted in a speech department when he himself used such a grotesque patois. He seemed to be defiantly demanding that his speech, and thus he himself, be accepted into the halls of learning.

He was also expressing a "thumb in the nose" attitude toward the white professors, as if to say: "Even speech professors know less about speech than I do. I can put one over on them. You have only to watch me do it!"

In a deeper sense Booker remained one with his father despite the disadvantage of his speech, since he was also "putting one over" on stupid white folks. He was wrapping himself in the cloak of his father's patois and thereby gaining a strength and virility which no doubt contributed to his romantic successes.

On a conscious level, his promiscuity was a series of competitive encounters with other men; on a deeper level, with white men; and ultimately, at a deeply unconscious level, with his father. He insisted on attributing his sexual triumphs to his use of the patois, but in truth he was simply an able and gifted seducer. He clung to his speech as the key to his successes, as he might have clung to a magic cloak or talisman.

For Booker and no doubt for many blacks, the patois involves a strengthening tie with one's forefathers who have by their wits persevered and overcome the white opponent.

Finally, Shakespeare demonstrates in *Henry V* and *Othello* that a man who is confident of his strength and powers may enter the arena of love disavowing verbal facility, that his passion, directness, and virility convey an eloquence unattainable by ordinary men. For the black man in the United States, the boudoir is a field of combat in which, rightfully or not, he is deemed by his society pre-eminent. His use of the patois, like Shakespeare's heroes, may dramatically highlight an already heroic presence.

# ⊟ VII ⊟

# The "Promise" of Education

## Weep for Our Children

A twelve-year-old boy, watching TV with his family, was engrossed in a dramatic work, which turned on a young man's discovery that he was color-blind. The younger watchers did not understand the concept "color-blindness." The twelve-year-old then, referring to the condition as "Daltonism" (the correct term), described how John Dalton had discovered the condition in himself and had first described it. He pointed out that it is sex-linked and differentiated congenital red-green color-blindness from other related conditions.

The boy's parents were pleased and surprised, but,

aware that he was an omnivorous reader, they regarded this display of knowledge as just another example of his accumulation of incidental information. They all but dismissed it from their minds and only later paid much attention to it, when the boy's school counselor told him that he was not very bright and that he should abandon aspirations for college and "work with his hands."

All his life the boy had shown his parents evidence of his above-average intellectual gifts, but his *performance* in school was always mediocre and they found themselves treating him as if he were a dull child in need of coaching and tutoring. Only when they consciously set their child's discourse on Daltonism against his counselor's recommendation that he work with his hands were they able to break the spell woven by the teachers' and their own anxiety.

Children are responsive to the expectations of their environment. They read clearly both the conscious and the unconscious message. While it is clear that the counselor's expectations and preconceptions of how black boys functioned intellectually prevented him from seeing this child's true capabilities, what is less obvious, but more important, was the parents' excessive concern that their son not be stupid. If they muster so much energy to keep him from performing poorly, then with his own logic he must conclude that they feel he is very close to being stupid or is very likely to perform poorly and that it is this stupidity, this poor performance, which represents the great danger to them. They reveal in this way their own imperfectly disguised expectation of the child, which parallels that of the counselor.

The unfortunate child finds himself in a world where even his own parents can barely see beyond the color of his skin. It is as if he yells and waves his arms but no one notices *him;* everyone sees only his dark cloak. The process of learning, a uniquely personal event under any circumstances, becomes for this child a lonely task, in which his triumphs pass unnoticed and any idle act may bring down a rain of admonition to do better, along with poorly concealed contempt.

The child is in danger of being what both parents and counselor might have been: stupid, ignorant, contemptible—and black. The very ordinary process of learning has vaulted him into the center of everyone's conflict, namely: Will I be smart, clean, clever, obedient, loved, successful, important, rich (and white), or will I be stupid, dirty, awkward, defiant, despised, and an unimportant, impoverished failure (who is black)?

He finds himself at the center of a storm so violent that he stands little chance of moving beyond it unaffected. And there is even less chance that his capacity to learn will remain fresh and broad. For him the long process of education is something akin to the trial of a long-distance runner who is occasionally peppered with buckshot; he may complete the race but it will take something out of him.

One of the keystones in white America's justification of its exploitation of black people is the assumption that black men are stupid. It is assumed that they cannot learn as much as a white man and therefore cannot assume positions of power and responsibility. (The essence of the concept of white supremacy is that every white man is inherently superior to every black man.) It is a vital piece of the American self-concept, for it has allowed the nation to grow fat off black men's labor and to bar them from even the meanest participation in the wealth they have produced. South Africa is merely America with the pretty tinsel ripped off.

So our black child has been raised by parents who have lived all their lives in these brackish waters, who may have held on to a perception of their own intelligence and capability but at great psychological expense. It is more likely, however, that the parents absorbed some of the poison of white society and to some extent they felt about themselves as their country felt about them. They may have fought against this concept and set out to prove that it was not true, unaware that they were driven to disprove it because in part they believed it. They may have projected the idea onto other black men saying: "Aren't they stupid?" or "Aren't they dumb niggers?"—all the while comforting themselves with that sad, sad comment: "I'm glad I'm different."

Such parents would no doubt say to their child: "You must be different also." And the child hears that he must be like his parents, dreading some blackness in himself which, he further hears, is associated with all the negative things said about black men.

The whole conflict at this level between black and white carries strong overtones of filth and cleanliness for the child—not too far removed in time from his earliest years, when such matters were of fundamental concern to him. It easily gets mixed with the moral injunctions of a few years before, when his parents humiliated him for

133

being dirty and praised him for being clean. And now he is asked to be clean (white), even though he is black. All the positive attributes, including cleverness, are associated with being good and clean, and his parents urge him in that direction. But they act as if they know he cannot be what they want him to be. His blackness carries so many implications which he must learn.

A black child was approached by a white child who rubbed his dark skin with her fingers and asked: "But how do you ever get clean?"

The concepts of cleanliness and orderliness and the joyful acquisition of knowledge are all related. Black children go to school and rapidly come to perceive the formal learning process as different, strange, unnatural, not meant for them, and not really relevant for them. The air they breathe, the water they drink, and the words they read all tell them that white people are smart and black people are dumb. And they could blot it all out and fight their way to intellectual distinction were it not for their parents. All messages are filtered through the child-parent relationship—and all have relevance only as they relate to that union. The child looks with clear eyes into the parent's heart and says: "Forget the world beyond. Tell me how you are, and that is how I will be, in my love for you." And he dashes away happy, shouting for all the world to hear: "I am black, dumb, and dirty," and to himself saying: "My love for her is boundless."

Schools are designed to train children to participate in the work of the society and to impart to them a certain attitude about the nation. The earliest schools taught the children of nobility to wage war and to govern. Only in relatively recent times has the work of the common man reached such complexity as to require special training. It is more than coincidence that in this country the growth of universal education has run parallel with the growth of industrialization and its need for more skilled laborers. Since 1865, black people have occupied a truly anomalous position in this country—unskilled agricultural laborers in an economy which has had a rapidly decreasing use for them. Moreover, they were rigorously excluded from participation in the wave of industrialization and were left, like buggy-whip makers, high and dry with no salable skill.

In spite of the yammering of naive observers, education has never offered a significant solution to the black man's dilemma in America. In the eyes of policy makers, education has always been meant to serve the pragmatic function of training people for work. If black men have not been allowed into the job markets, then the educational opportunities denied them by the nation generally have reflected that fact. The point is that they continue to be regarded as a class of illiterate laborers who are bothersome and underfoot because the nation now sees no way to profitably exploit them. Moreover, it has not decided what to do with them. There was something orderly and proper about blacks laboring in the cotton fields and America is loath to relinquish this idea. Although education may in the long run be an important instrument for black people, children may have clearer vision when they see the classroom as immediately irrelevant. Their vision is clearer than that of men who plead for black people to become educated in a land which views all blacks as bondsmen temporarily out of bondage.

These are the poisonous waters through which black children must find their way.

Having made it to school, the child encounters that reluctant instrument of the establishment, the teacher. In such an encounter one is at a loss to decide who is more deserving of pity, the children or the teacher, who may have nursed an idealism longer than most people, who sees it eroding in the face of hypocrisy, who slowly comes to view her task as the crushing of spirit and the dulling of eyes.

Teachers are in low repute in America in large measure because they have no independent atmosphere in which to exercise their calling. The rigid control of teachers, curriculum, and budget by generally small-minded governing bodies again reflects the essential purpose of the schools—which is to serve the immediate economic ends of those who control them. Out of the same pragmatic thinking which produced the trade school and the commercial school has lately come the tracking program, a system for selecting one of several programs for students based on the child's performance and test results. These programs have operated to launch white children into college and to provide mindless "busy work" for black children until they are seventeen.

A black educator, a specialist in instructional materials, insists that, in spite of all other factors, an imaginative approach to learning could keep the spark alive in black children. Since the cost of such materials and training is modest, he said, to deny the children these aids is to deny them the union card of a high school or college education, without which employment these days is a sometime thing.

No one is more aware of this bizarre state of affairs than the teacher. It makes no difference if the teacher is white in a white suburban school, manning the ramparts against black invaders, or in fact a dedicated white teacher in a black ghetto. The white teacher knows as well as her black counterpart that the general quality of education in this country is rather seedy and the training children get is geared to mediocrity. The teacher would doubtless welcome an opportunity to participate in the development of an enlightened and intellectually vigorous citizenry. But the slow disenchantment of teachers, as they see the true dimensions of their task, contributes heavily, we feel, to the profusion of "bad teachers"—bitter, resentful beings who arrive at school each day with a baggage of contempt, ridicule, and sometimes open hatred for their tender charges. Frustrated idealists make poor guardians of a nation's youth.

The black parent approaches the teacher with the great respect due a person of learning. The soaring expectations which are an important part of the parent's feelings find substance in the person of the teacher. Here is the person who can do for this precious child all the wonderful things a loving parent cannot. The child is admonished to obey the teacher as he would his parents and the teacher is urged to exercise parental prerogatives, including beating. In this the parent yields up his final unique responsibility, the protection of his child against another's aggression. The child is placed in the teacher's hands to do with as she sees fit, with the sole requirement that she teach him. The meaning of this gift is not lost on the teacher, who is alternately touched by the parent's trust and staggered by the responsibility, for the teacher knows best of all that much has gone on before she gets the child and knows that, even as the parent urges her not to spare the rod, that same parent is telling volumes about the life that child has led up to this moment. The parent tells of a child both beloved and beaten, of a child taught to look for pain from even those who cherish him most, of a child who has come to feel that beatings are right and proper for him, and of a child whose view of the world, however gently it persuades him to act toward others, decrees for him that he is to be driven by the infliction of pain.

Pity that child.

Beating in child-rearing actually has its psychological roots in slavery and even yet black parents will feel that, just as they have suffered beatings as children, so it is right that their children be so treated. This kind of physical subjugation of the weak forges early in the mind of the child a link with the past and, as he learns the details of history, with slavery per se.

Beyond these early years rise the fantastic promise of "higher education." When all is taken into account, the proliferation of educational institutions for Negroes, along with the large number of black people attending these schools, has been a remarkable phenomenon. In view of the fact that this development has occurred primarily in the South, where early education has been poor, the phenomenon takes on even more unusual dimensions. When finally one adds the sobering fact that even with education the fate of black people in the South has been dismal, eagerness for learning on the part of black people becomes a curiosity worthy of study.

Any explanation of this drive toward learning must take into account the dearth of alternative modes of expression. Black people have always had reason to be skeptical of success in other fields of endeavor, for, if success were measured in terms of goods acquired, those goods could easily be taken away. Education was said to be "something no one can ever take away from you." It was therefore one of the very few areas of accomplishment where a level of "success" could be attained within a special Jim Crow arena of competition.

Black merchants were nonexistent; black politicians floated in a curious nonexistence, representing merely a cluster of black people and far removed from the seats of power. Black men were left pretty much to the fields of entertainment and education as areas in which advancement was possible.

Education had an ennobling quality which set one apart from the more common people. Just as white garments distinguished an upper-class nineteenth-century Korean from his brethren of the soil, and as the bound feet of upper-class Chinese women indicated that they had no need to walk as did the common people—so did the possession of an education separate a learned black man from his less fortunate brothers. It was of special significance, too, because of the all-pervading notion that blacks were ignorant and stupid. The learned black man found himself isolated by society generally as one who was "different," an "exception"—which was to say that his accomplishment was set to one side and the prevailing view that all black people were ignorant continued in full force.

This view fostered his own alienation from his group as well, offering him rewards not for his scholarship but often on the basis of his being a curiosity, much as one pays to see a seal play the piano. If, then, he is to capitalize on his efforts, he must accept this role and affirm the general view that he is an exception and that in fact no blacks can learn. And this continues to be the dilemma of the black intellectual—fighting to maintain a tie with his people but paid for being so curiously different from the mass of them.

America, by virtue of its incredible rate of economic growth, has had a constant need for men in increasing numbers and with increasing skills to fully exploit its potential and realize its promise. As a result, it has been able to say to every man—learn, and your skills will take you further than you ever imagined in your wildest dreams. There is no ceiling for you; this is truly the land of opportunity. This was no illusion, but every thoughtful man must now ask himself why the vast reservoir of black manpower was excluded from these opportunities. Why were the burgeoning factories of the North peopled by immigrants from Europe brought to this country at some risk and expense? Why were the lands of the West opened to all men of the soil save the most accomplished lovers of land—black men? With education the magic key to all this land's riches, why were only those with fair skin allowed to have it?

We propose that it was the economic usefulness of

slavery in the period when cotton was king which in turn gave rise to the moral, religious, and psychological justification of the enslavement of blacks. Moral justification followed economic necessity and black Americans were viewed as subhumans designed for laboring in the fields. The incidental freeing of blacks after the Civil War was followed by a "conservative" backlash in which the newly freed slaves were abandoned to the tender mercies of their former owners while the main commercial business of America moved ahead under a gathering impetus. Negroes drifted into a "nonexistence" which they still occupy.

To have maintained a fervent interest in education and a belief in the rewards of learning required a major act of faith. Black people in America have been nothing if not idealists and devotees of the American dream. It is a source of wonder where such unending faith had its origins.

Whatever its source, faith in education has been a disappearing commodity among the most fortunate black beneficiaries of the educational system. Black intellectuals are a disenchanted lot. They have overcome incredible odds and have performed the impossible. They have had to cling to their own view of themselves amid violent contrary winds, holding fast only to ties that feel familiar and right, however strange those ties may seem to others.

A brilliant high school student was awarded a scholarship to a prestigious eastern school. Despite the enthusiastic encouragement of friends and family, he chose rather a small

Negro college of modest reputation located in the South. He finally explained:

"If I go East, I can never come back."

"Back" was to home, family, friends, and a brotherhood of black people.

Black people feel bound to the concept of equality. It is a belief which allows them to live. It cannot have merely an occasional hortatory meaning for black Americans— it must be seen as a universal truth. No other conviction can sustain black people in this country. It is absorbed in childhood and built on the child's conception of fairness. Public pronouncements of every kind can find a responsive affirmation in black breasts if they only include the word "equality." The idea of all men's equality lies at the deepest level of the black man's conception of social organization. Slavery and the post-Civil War experience have made this concept dear indeed.

It extends from the broad social meanings to its implementation in everyday life. Black children are acutely sensitive to the undemocratic formation of "exclusive" groups and social bodies. This conviction finds support in the concept of brotherhood. We are not only brothers but brothers keenly aware of our equal status.

But the belief in equality produces conflict when the black child is introduced to intellectual striving, competition, and the evaluation of his innate abilities. Some youngsters are far brighter than their brethren. When their gifts allow them to soar beyond the modest accomplishments of the others, the binding requirement of equality is encountered and problems arise. One may feel that to outstrip one's brothers is a wicked thing. To an nounce oneself as an exception is to bring calumny down on one's head. To say that one is smarter is to say that one's brothers are dumber, and that is a difficult thing for a black student.

Those with great intellectual gifts develop the technique of denying or minimizing them. A striking example of this occurred in treatment.

A young woman revealed her intellectual gifts only gradually. She told over a period of weeks, bit by bit, that she had achieved a distinguished academic record and finally that she had been given numerous intelligence tests and on all of them had "gone off the top," which is to say she was gifted to a degree that the tests were not calibrated to measure. Her intelligence could only be estimated.

In one session this bright woman described a major Caribbean island as located in the Mediterranean. Questioned repeatedly, she stuck to her mistake. Finally the therapist suggested that she knew better and that she had made the error for some other purpose. She laughed and said that her great dread during treatment was the prospect of finding that she was brighter than the therapist and that from her earliest school years she had tried to obscure her knowledge and to make herself appear less gifted than she was.

She was a vigorous champion of the cause of black people and found the idea of an intellectual aristocracy repugnant to her. Although she welcomed the challenge to match wits with white opponents and in fact rose to magnificent heights in such intellectual combat, she laid down her arms when confronted by a black antagonist.

Her situation is typical of many bright black students. Intellectual achievement is regarded as elevating oneself to a higher plane and removing oneself from the black brotherhood. The tie to blackness here is rarely perceived as the militant self-conscious pride of being black but rather as the deeper, sweeter, more profound ties to beloved figures of childhood.

Such a conflict partly explains why so many gifted black students achieve academic distinction but fail to fulfill their vocational promise. Accomplishment in school can be seen as simply carrying out the wishes of the family, whereas accomplishment in a career may represent a major move beyond the family—a move to another level out of contact with those whose love is life itself.

The scholar finds himself especially torn, driven to excel academically by the ambitions of family, yet pulled to maintain an all-important equality with those same beloved ones. He yields most often to the stronger force— the leveling effect of love.

The unique quality of this conflict arises from the strength of the call for equality. All Americans feel committed to the principle of "all men, created equal," but it does not occupy a central position in their view of their place in America. It is a case of "All men are born equal, but white men are more equal than anyone else."

For black men the concept of equality functions as an ideological bulwark against the pervasive idea that Negroes are stupid. The black man clings to it as one of the nation's highest principles. By calling upon Americans to respond to a statement of national conscience and by reminding them of their declared ideals, he is defending himself against the institutionalized depreciation of black people in this country. This devotion to principles, ideals, and conscience marks all blacks with a certain idealism which seems inappropriate in so atavistic a land.

There is a separate and curious effect that American attitudes have had on the academic aspirations of black children which is related to the sexual roles adopted by boys and girls. It has often been observed that black parents push girls in the family to remain in school and in many ways encourage them and make higher education more accessible to them. On the other hand, the same family may discourage its sons, urge them to drop out of school, and make it difficult for them to obtain an education. The reasons are not immediately obvious.

Mrs. J., who lived in the South in the 1920's, had eight children. She prodded her four daughters to obtain higher education and in spite of the family's extremely low income she made sure that the girls had some college instruction. Mrs. J. was a domestic and earned a precarious living unaided by public assistance. Her sons, she felt, "could look out for themselves," and when they were very young she told them of her need for whatever money they could earn. As a result, the oldest son quit school at fourteen and the others by the age of sixteen. All contributed to help the girls continue their education.

Here the rationale is clearer than most. Living in the South, Mrs. J. was concerned about the physical safety and protection she could offer her children. She admonished her sons to avoid conflict with white people and it would be blessing enough for her if they avoided the hostile physical encounters which could place their lives in jeopardy.

With her daughters it was a different story. Her aim was to protect them from the sexual exploitation they might suffer if they were forced to work as domestics. She knew that in the South an attractive young black girl who worked in a white household was in considerable danger of being used sexually by the men of the house. She also knew that the weapon used to bend the girl to their will was the economic threat of being fired if she refused to submit. To free the girls from this certain development, the mother sought to give them economic freedom through the education which allowed them all to become schoolteachers. As teachers, the girls would possess a dignity and an autonomy they could never have as black domestics in the South.

But even this strategy did not always succeed. The story is heard from many lips of white school administrators threatening to fire black teachers if they spurned sexual advances. If this pressure could be applied at so elevated and public a level, it must have been common indeed in the narrow secret world of the domestic servant.

For the boys, the world was quite a different place. It was exceedingly dangerous, and the first task was to develop a style of life which allowed one to survive. Avoid fights with white boys, particularly avoid gangs of white toughs, and speak with deference to white men. If one learned what situations to *avoid,* one could achieve as much safety as the South could afford a black man. Those slow to learn might not live very long in any event. The lessons were swift and cruel.

A boy lived with his uncle, whom he adored. Their particular pleasure was spending Saturdays in town together. One such afternoon while walking along a street, they met a white man with his son, who was larger than the dark child. Without ado the white man kicked the black child and ordered his son to beat him up. The white boy beat him thoroughly while the uncle stood aside and sadly watched the proceedings.

In later life the black boy, now a man, said it took many years to forgive his uncle and even more to understand how painful it must have been for him, how wretched a life he led which required him, probably under penalty of death, to watch a child he loved being beaten and to be unable to raise a hand in protest. That boy is now a man and there are no words to convey the depth of his hatred for white men. But he carries on his daily life without a hint of rage.

If the boys learned this lesson, they learned something about the male role as well. For black men in America, in the old South and the new North, masculinity carries overtones of violence. One must either deal with and placate a violent white man or as a man defend oneself with violence against murderous threats. To position oneself, then, in relation to aggression became a vital part of masculinity. The man who fought when threatened and lived to tell the tale became a man who had dealt successfully with truly manly things—a man among men, a man of violence, a man who held his manhood dear, and though his life was likely to be brief had laid hold of the essential task of men and particularly black men—survival and opposition to the foe. And although we have described earlier how they terrified the Negro community and in a sense provided a negative model for "nice families," such men (bad niggers) had profound importance for the Negro community. They provided the measure of manhood for all black men and stood in ultimate masculine opposition to the feminine counterpart who sought protection from the foe by turning to education.

Thus any man who turned from violent confrontation of the white enemy and instead followed academic pursuits would have to feel deep inside, in his heart of hearts, that he had retreated from the battle. It was his secret, this cowardice, and there was an emptiness where his manhood might have been.

This played a part in the division of roles in girls who went to school and boys who dropped out. For in one sense school was seen by black families in a very special way. Beset on all sides by a cruel enemy, school was often primarily a refuge—a place of safety for those who were to be protected—and in a sense it was a case of women and children first.

These attitudes do not complete the catalogue of black people's feelings about school and schooling but they are important. They continue to play an important part to this day because the violence to which blacks are exposed in this country is faced by no other group of people in America. If school is seen as a refuge from the white aggressor, and if the black family places its women and children within such safe confines, and if the men then turn to face the enemy—*pray show me that critic of the "weak" Negro family!*

If the critics do not understand, then one may say that such everyday heroics are not performed for the critics' sake; fortunately they are carried out for love of man for woman and both for child.

And if school is regarded as of secondary importance and as having little relevance in the heat of battle where men are called to war, pray tell us who wages war on black people? One can only feel dismay if a man lays deadly siege to your house and then criticizes you for not going about innocent daily chores.

Such are the profound influences of American racism on the black man's involvement in education. In his mind school is converted from an instrument of social mobility to a place of refuge. The roles of black boys and girls are changed from potential participants in the fullness of America to females to be protected and men to face the enemy. It is a greater source of wonder that black children choose to learn at all.

Such are the factors that make academic achievement difficult for dark students: loving but untrusting parents, discouraged teachers, institutional opposition to a learned black community, and a state of war that has both historical roots and a contemporary reality. When in spite of these barriers a student surfaces as an academician, the passage through these dark places has left its mark. He steps onstage to put his skill to work in a nation and an economy which has blocked his progress at every step and which yet offers him serious obstacles.

The systematic discrimination against black academicians and intellectuals is a dreary tale well told by many voices. Let us add only this: The paths beyond scholarly excellence may lead to positions of power in government, in industry, or in the administrative hierarchy of major educational institutions. But the black man who has breached so many barriers to achieve academic status must at this writing realize that further doors are open to all save him. His is a blind alley. His achievements are circumscribed by the same impediments of discrimination as are those of his less gifted brother.

If education truly freed the brother from this peculiarly American latter-day bondage, the transition from black to white might actually be approached by means of the refinement of skills. But there is no prospect of this and no one realizes it more keenly that the black intellectual.

A distinguished black educator was sent overseas to organize the educational system for a sizable population. The area in which he was billeted offered many scenic views and he took a walk one afternoon with his camera to take photographs. He came upon a small village and walked down the main road. A jeep with several American military policemen roared up and the occupants spoke impatiently: "Over there! Over there!" pointing to a side road which they meant he should take.

He asked why, and they answered: "Colored soldiers go on that side!"

Furious, he went where they indicated and discovered that the village housed mainly prostitutes who had been neatly divided for blacks on one side and whites on the other. The military policemen had thought he was seeking prostitutes and made sure he realized that their wares were segregated. The same man, as it happened, did a commendable job of reorganization and on his return to the United States found himself in line for a promotion to a major administrative position, one carrying great power and prestige. His training and experience fitted him perfectly for the job. He was taken aside, however, and the explanation given was that the region was simply "not ready" for a Negro to occupy so sensitive and so powerful a position.

It may not be appropriate to feel pity for so gifted and so fortunate a man, but we know that he does not share the affection his colleagues feel for this social system. He must know that his area of function is sharply limited by his blackness. He knows that there is no substantial difference between him and the lowliest black laborer save the grandeur of the arena in which they play out their lives. Both are held in check, both are restricted, both are called upon to embrace a society which views them with contempt.

Within the space of a few months this man had heard the harsh voice of his country telling him first which whores were not for him and next what power he must not have. He would surely have been hard put to differentiate between the laborer and the intellectual, at least if they are black and live in America.

And this precisely is the dilemma of the black intellectual. Now most of all he sees no difference whatsoever between himself and his poorer brother as they both relate themselves to the nation. The crux of the issue is that he alone sees their common bond. Others see him as only incidentally black, as an intellectual who happens to be a Negro, as a white black man. His poorer brethren cheer him on and vicariously relish his triumphs, but if he is too long in their company they become uncomfortable and wonder what they should say. They sense that he has no home with them any longer. The white community sees him as "different" from his darker brothers and capable of being viewed as one of their own when such meets their convenience. The net effect is an alienation from his roots with no substitute available. He cannot go forward and cannot go back. He may try to bind himself to blackness and voice the spirit of dark people; he may attack the white man, taking up the sword for his people; he may try in a thousand ways to become engaged in the battle, but always he enters from the outside and his contribution is that of an outsider. As the giants move toward battle, his is the voice of the bystander begging for engagement.

The black intellectual must accept his exclusion from this battle. If he is called by his brothers, he will leap to their aid. If they fail to call, he will continue to pursue his version of truth. He cannot force himself on them. He must be primarily devoted to truth. If the white man challenges him, the black scholar must demolish him with truth. His sword is his science, and only when he has finally fashioned a formidable weapon can it be put to use for his people and only when he limits his thrust to his special view of the world.

Thus it would be a pity if black scholars were swept up in a tide of anti-intellectualism. It would be understandable, of course, since education has been yearned for by the masses and has proven a failure. We can understand their turning away as well as their mounting distrust of the complexities of modern affairs. Why shouldn't black masses look upon such complexities with a jaundiced eye? They have always meant exclusion. Moreover, if education is necessary for participation in national affairs and education is denied him, the black man sees accurately if he sees education as an arm of that depriving white majority. No, his attitude is justified.

Such an attitude cannot be justified, however, by the black scholar. He has made his way past the impediments and finds himself now armed with modern science. To turn away from this opportunity shared by so few of his brothers is to deprive them of an arm they need desperately.

Our thesis is that black people are locked in a life struggle, and the black mothers all over America who urge their children: "Get some knowledge in your head; that's something no one can take away from you," are telling them a great deal about a vicious social order which rapes and exploits them and in which only a black man's ideas are safe from the white predator. The message is not lost on the children.

# VIII

# Mental Illness and Treatment

### If a Black Man Comes Unglued

Fundamentally one wonders why there should be anything singular about a Negro's mental troubles. We would like to answer that right away. There is nothing reported in the literature or in the experience of any clinician known to the authors that suggests that black people *function* differently psychologically from anyone else. Black men's mental functioning is governed by the same *rules* as that of any other group of men. Psychological principles understood first in the study of white men are true no matter what the man's color.

A graduate student in social work took as his project a study of the principles governing the psychological growth and development of black people.

His misguided chauvinism made it difficult for him to see that while the *experiences* of black people in this country are unique, the *principles* of psychological functioning are by definition universal.

We do not wish to suggest that we are similarly naive, but rather that the unique experience of black men is a constant factor influencing growth and activity and is frequently a focal point upon which basic principles are seen to act.

The problems encountered by emotionally troubled blacks are by no means confined to the black people.

A pair of six-year-old twins was seen in a child guidance clinic because of suspected severe mental disorder. They showed evidence of gross neglect, and attention naturally turned to the mother. She was a poorly groomed black woman of thirty-two. She had five other children and had never been married. A worker who visited the home described it as chaotic. The mother seemed ignorant of the most fundamental ideas of child-rearing. She seemed dull and uncomprehending of the investigation that had begun. After a case conference on the problem, the white clinicians concluded that this woman, who had a wretched childhood in the rural South and little schooling, was culturally retarded because of her early life, and they thought that a program of home aides and instruction in home management would move her toward more effective mothering.

In reality, the woman was psychotic and in need of intensive treatment. This important fact was overlooked by sympathetic clinicians who were so impressed by her dismal childhood that they wanted to help her "catch up." It also reflects a clouded vision of Negro life in which many white clinicians are so impressed by the alarming world in which black people live that they are unable to bring the individual pathology into clear focus.

White clinicians may unconsciously withdraw from an intimate knowledge of a black man's life because placing themselves in the position of the patient, even mentally, is too painful. Since such an intimate knowledge of the patient is vital to diagnosis and treatment, in its absence the patient suffers.

Black therapists have a difficult path to travel, since their discipline and long training have taken place primarily in a white milieu. There are few black psychiatrists of national reputation and in any event the major theoreticians and innovators in the field have been white. These factors, coupled with the black clinician's own inevitable problems of identification, make it difficult for him to be comfortable with his blackness and to feel sufficiently in command of his own destiny to reach out a hand to another sufferer. Understand: *difficult*—by no means impossible. One has only to look at the rapidly increasing numbers of black clinicians, skilled, well trained, and working in the field, to see that it is possible.

We only say that, as in other areas of personal growth, expansion, and development in this country, all such growth is hedged about with more hazards for black men.

If such hazards have led the black clinician to treat his black patient with the tentative, hands-off attitude of a reluctant white therapist, then the patient is no better served. It points to the futility of simply providing black therapists for troubled people, black or white. The black therapist ought to be available, but it needs to be recognized that his real usefulness will come into play only when he begins to grapple with his own feelings about being black, ineffective, and victimized in a powerful white nation.

In addition to the problems contributed by the therapist, there are certain confusing elements made more confusing by the fluid lines of social class in this country. The clinician may find it difficult to avoid placing the black patient in a class which has in his own mind certain "givens" that apply to all its members.

A black laborer who comes to the consultation room shabbily dressed, behaving in an awkward manner, and speaking in an ungrammatical southern patois, says many things about himself in the way he looks and acts. But how *he is* may by no means approximate the images stimulated in the mind of the therapist. "Lower-class laborer" may mean one thing and "lower-class Negro laborer" may mean something else again, and neither set of images may have any relation to the unique life of the man who sits across the desk.

With another group of patients, some black and white apologists would deny that there are black scoundrels. Well, in fact, there are, and they are no better served when clinicians close their eyes to rascality.

In sum, let us enter a plea for *clinical* clinicians who

can distinguish unconscious depression from conscious despair, paranoia from adaptive wariness, and who can tell the difference between a sick man and a sick nation.

Miss Y. was first seen during an acute psychotic episode. When it subsided she settled into a precarious marginal state of chronic anxiety and suspiciousness. Minor stress would cause the development of another brief but full-blown psychotic episode. As treatment continued, the episodes occurred with less frequency and the quality of the marginal intervals became clear. At best her life was hellish. She felt persecuted by family and co-workers, misunderstood by friends, and neglected by men. Surprisingly, she held a demanding job entailing considerable responsibility. Her employer thought so highly of her work that he willingly put up with her periodic absences and irritable outbursts on the job. She was diligent and conscientious in the extreme, and when her life in general turned into a nightmare her work seemed largely spared. In fact, she seemed most normal on the job. As a child she had medical problems which necessitated many months of hospitalization up to her tenth year. During this period physical movement was limited for months at a time. The child's suffering prompted her parents to indulge her in an unfortunately too infantile way for too long. She became a demanding, spoiled child. But she was bright in school and ambitious, and in her early twenties obtained a good job.

Her earlier physical problems had left her with a significant deformity, which imposed some limitations on her relationship with men. She had several affairs, however, and it was in association with an acute disappointment in one such love relationship that the whole cycle of psychosis and troubled intervals began.

Miss Y. was a paranoid schizophrenic whose life style

and good relationship with the therapist were able to provide him with a long, studied view of a chronic schizophrenic woman adjusting to work and the other demands of life.

In her work situation certain symptoms came to the fore in a manner which may be instructive for us. She felt on one occasion that she (the only black person at her rather high level) was being discriminated against and being denied a promotion simply because she was black. When asked for specific evidence of this, she said that other workers less skillful than she and with shorter tenure on the job were being promoted while she remained at the same job. She admitted that there were others with approximately the same tenure who were not promoted, but she insisted that they were not particularly capable anyway and ought to be kept back whereas *she* should be promoted.

The therapist agreed with her on the general prevalence of racial prejudice in work situations and added that it seemed more of a problem at higher job levels. She was asked about other evidence of racial discrimination and what remedies if any were available to employees. She said that all her superiors were vicious, prejudiced bastards who were likely to frustrate any mechanism available for the presentation of employee grievances. As other examples of prejudice she recalled a co-worker who had been very friendly but who lately was cool and disinclined even to speak to her. The nature of her job was such that certain workers would consult her on details of their work. She complained that lately they arranged to consult other members of the staff.

Such examples prompted the therapist to raise the question of her illness. She had, after all, behaved rather strangely at work on more than one occasion and her co-workers knew that she had been hospitalized for her emotional ailments. Could it be that they were afraid of her because of her symptoms?

She thought for a long while and then burst into laughter. "Those bastards are not too well put together themselves! I'd probably scare the hell out of them if I said 'Boo!' And they must be really tied up in knots over what to do with this crazy nigger woman who's got such a big job!"

She laughed herself breathless, and as she wiped away the tears the therapist felt tears start in his own eyes, but from a more solemn source than the tears of the laughing woman who needed to be laughed with but who needed also to be wept for.

This unhappy woman had to deal not only with the prejudices of her co-workers toward the mentally ill and toward women but with the additional factor of her being black as well. She had to separate her own pathological suspicions from the reactions of fellow workers, which were troublesome enough but, as she observed, also compounded by her being a "crazy nigger."

Paranoid people not only are given to seeing dangers which do not exist but on a realistic level are inclined to be more sensitive to the motives of people around them. Thus with the onset of her illness this woman was no doubt more keenly attuned to the feelings of racial prejudice in her co-workers and what had previously passed unnoticed then became an unbearable, wide-ranging assault upon her by all her co-workers throughout the work day. And the chances are that in large measure she was right.

In an agony of persecution she once called a civil rights organization, asking that her employers be investigated and a stop put to the racial persecution they inflicted on their employees. She was told that the matter would be "looked into" and nothing more was heard about it. Later, in a more sober moment, she observed that they probably thought she was crazy, considering the way she carried on over the telephone, but didn't they realize that whether she was crazy or not those bastards might still be prejudiced and that there might be something a civil rights organization could do to tone down the more blatant discrimination?

Here again she touches on a significant matter. For a black man survival in America depends in large measure on the development of a "healthy" cultural paranoia. He must maintain a high degree of suspicion toward the motives of every white man and at the same time never allow this suspicion to impair his grasp of reality. It is a demanding requirement and not everyone can manage it with grace. In defense of the civil rights organization, one must say that they could not possibly pursue the complaints of racial discrimination raised by every black paranoid; such would be literally impossible, for with rare exceptions every paranoid black man is troubled about white persecution. Such concerns may be by no means central in their psychopathology but are a significant and vigorously verbalized source of pain.

Of all the varieties of functional psychosis, those that include paranoid symptoms are by far the most prevalent among black people. The frequency of paranoid symptoms is significantly greater among mentally ill blacks than it is among mentally ill whites.

We must also say that, given the difficult circumstances of her early life, Miss Y. would doubtless have developed a paranoid psychosis no matter what her racial experience, but being black in America meant that her environment demanded a certain paranoid posture of her regardless of her inner psychic structure. Her society made her illness itself an exquisitely painful thing and a misery which offers no respite. Finally, it made treatment more difficult, since, after all, who can really tell where her delusions end and reality begins in this mad, mad land?

Miss S. came for treatment confused, anxious, and depressed. A professional woman in her early thirties, she felt that she had always been neurotic, but she was particularly troubled now about the possibility that her moodiness, erratic behavior, and occasional poor performance jeopardized her work. Most of her colleagues were white and there was a fierce competition among them for advancement. She sometimes felt that she had been advanced far beyond her capabilities and that any critical examination of her work would cause her to be fired. She connected this feeling with being an orphan and explained that she had never known her natural mother. She had been told that her mother was an unmarried college girl who abandoned her in a distant town. Her adoptive mother had taken her, a sick newborn, and had raised her. The adoptive mother, while taking great pleasure in her pretty little girl, was herself quite disreputable. During the girl's childhood, this woman married once and entered into numerous liaisons, some of them most casual. She was given to long, roaring alcoholic binges and in her later years became increasingly paranoid. She was finally confined to a mental institution when the girl was sixteen and died there some fifteen years later.

Some of Miss S.'s earliest memories were of being taken

by her "mother" to a local tavern where she sat on the bar and chatted with the clientele. She suspected in later years that a good many of her mother's liaisons were based more on immediate financial considerations than on mutual fondness. The mother turned on the child at times and scratched her face, saying that she was too pretty to be so vicious and too fair for so black a heart. In spite of this inauspicious beginning, the child did well in school, obtained scholarships, and with a consistently high performance moved into and up in the job market. She had a long history of ill-fated affairs but had never felt the closeness and trust that would allow her to marry.

Soon treatment began to center on her low self-esteem and chronic depression, which were fundamentally related to her having been abandoned by her natural mother into the hands of an erratic and often cruel adoptive mother. She could utter the lamentation of the orphan: "My own mother threw me away. Of what use can I be? Who can love me?"

And yet it was her status as an orphan and the fact that she did *not* know her true parents which made it possible for her to distinguish herself in her career. As an orphan, knowing from her earliest years that she had no blood relationship to her adoptive mother, she was able psychologically to separate herself. She could imagine that her *real* parents were grand, glorious lovers who because of some tragic turn of fate had to abandon their beloved child. She literally thought of herself as a princess whom circumstance had decreed must be reared in unfortunate circumstances. These fantasies allowed her to get through her early years with good cheer, but with the death of her adoptive mother the whole airy framework of fantasy tumbled down and she again felt lost, abandoned, and depressed.

A parent's essential and fundamental purpose, beyond assuring the child's survival, is to provide an interpretation of the society to the child. The parent is the culture bearer and must act as a funnel through which the nature of the social system is brought to bear on the child in his earliest years. For life is ineffective unless its strengths are developed in the particular ways in which society tests newcomers. Thus the child first encounters his world-to-be in the person of the parent. Ideally, the love of the parent parallels the approval of the state, both giving praise to acts which please them. Likewise, the parent's punishment should properly parallel the response of the community to acts it finds offensive. By these means (not to ignore the influence of growth and its complexity) the child is to reach adulthood with an emotional equipment tested and in fact developed in contact with the blessings and curses he may expect from society.

If we accept the primacy of this principle, then the child's psychological growth and interaction with his parents and siblings, his psychosexual development, the amalgam of his physiology and psyche, and all the wonders of the youthful maturation of his mind can be seen within a common context. It is a trial, a preparation for the world, a special setting in which the growth of his psychological apparatus will unfold within a setting similar to that in which later it will be required to function.

The blind efficiency of the system is a source of wonder when all goes well. The parent, familiar with the social order, functions as a lens, focusing the essentials of the social order on the child. But at best the lens is neutral, conveying the truth, however grim, of the world the child will come to know. And if the parent is a poor instrument, the child will see the world distorted by the parent's own dim vision.

The point is that, except for an unusual set of circumstances, Miss S. would have owed not only her life to her adoptive mother but also her view of the world and her view of herself. But because the mother was so grossly unacceptable and because the child was an orphan and knew that there was no blood tie—and because of the youngster's own innate gifts—she was able to reject the mother as an interpreter of society and fashion an independent conception of the world.

As a result, we are privileged to see the operation of some important factors in child development. Not only is it important that the parents convey an unconscious message to the child, and not only is the way they communicate and in fact the content of the message crucial —but a vitally important datum in the child's understanding of his world is the information he gains by learning of the role his parent occupies in the society.

What value does society place on this human being who represents the child's only link with that society? If the group places a high value on that person, this surely will influence the child's self-perception. If the social order views the parent with contempt (when a father is referred to as a "boy"), this too represents a message to the child from society.

The remarkable career of this orphan girl shows us what is possible if the child can avoid the stultifying oppressive messages of depreciation beamed toward him by his society. This child was able to dismiss all the negative signals and fashion (in fantasy) a loving, educated mother, black like herself, who had to abandon her beloved child because of some tragedy. In fantasy the mother loved her and wanted the best for her and, in response, the child bloomed.

Consider, then, the mass implications of an ethnically distinct group which is oppressed and viewed with contempt by the majority. Consider the stunting of ambition and drive and the mounting pressure on all sides to cast aside a burden which blights whole generations at a time.

In an earlier discussion we spoke of the proneness of black women to depressive, self-depreciatory attitudes. Those black people who succumb to social ambition find themselves in a similar precarious psychological position.

In the course of treatment a young woman who had achieved a responsible position described her family as distinguished. Her father was a prominent man and she tended to follow in his path as she gained one honor after another. Her mother was a housewife with limited aspirations and the father was a self-made man of modest origins. There was therefore no history or tradition of distinction.

She had a neurotic attachment to her father which influenced the pattern of her life and her view of her family. But she saw herself as coming from distinguished origins. She spoke as if a tradition of leadership existed and as if she, born into this tradition, had the obligation to make appropriate contributions.

She was a social climber and went to great pains to mix with people she thought important. She made decisions about her home furnishings on the basis of the recommendations of an expensive decorator whom she knew was engaged by a prominent person. She dressed, spoke, and generally carried herself as if she were of important lineage.

Her situation can be duplicated a thousand times over in black and white settings. No matter where such a preoccupation with status is seen it is usually an unfortunate burden. Such people have a feeling of personal bankruptcy together with a longing for praise. They attach themselves to the abstract concept of "family" and in this way seek to live out their dreams. It is a device which flies in the face of reality, even when it is employed by moneyed Anglo-Saxons. It cannot serve the purpose intended because the individual so much in need of this praise has generally made little or no contribution to earn it.

The aspirations of the black social climber are particularly dangerous. The accomplishments of kin may be solid and praiseworthy, but, because black people are involved, the community may withhold its praise. By far the greater problem lies in the alternatives, once a black man takes such a position. If he abandons his own personal striving for accomplishment and in so doing admits personal bankruptcy, then any failure of the "family" to meet his needs for status leaves him on the brink of despair. His esteem can drop to dangerous levels. He becomes not simply a man who has accomplished little but a black ne'er-do-well and wastrel. In his own mind he identifies himself with black irresponsibility and foolishness so celebrated in American story and song.

In effect, the bottom is very much deeper when a black man falls. A pit has been dug for him and he thus places himself and his self-esteem at great hazard when he clings to false handholds.

The story is told that Malcolm X was speaking to a campus audience at a large university when a Negro intellectual shot a series of hostile, virulent remarks at him. Malcolm answered with a question:

"Do you know what they call a Negro scholar, Ph.D., professor?"

"No."

"A nigger!'

With this, perhaps, the issue can rest. No one can improve upon Malcolm.

The man was very young, wore dark glasses, and walked with a hurried, businesslike gait. Everything about him said that he was up to no good. There was a too naive look on his open face. He seemed to be searching to find what the therapist wanted to hear.

His mother had made the appointment in a syrupy, cloying voice which spelled out his misdeeds while establishing that such a refined person as she and as refined a person as she knew the therapist to be would both naturally recoil from her son's misbehavior. However, the voice seemed to urge that the young man's problems be dealt with.

He was the youngest of three children, all of whom were bright and gratifying to their teachers. The father, a meek, clerical type, was dominated by the vigorous mother, who was pious and active in community works. She had long felt in a despairing way that her youngest child was her greatest trial. The boy had always been defiant and rebellious. For a while, as a preadolescent, he submitted to his mother's display of him as a good example of pious upbringing. When he broke away, he became more violent. He engaged in organized theft at the age of thirteen, heading his own gang. He drank heavily, attempted to establish himself as a pimp, and began using hard narcotics all before the age of fifteen. In spite of his desultory attendance, he was bright enough to get average grades in high school and with his mother's influence managed to be accepted by a university. There he was a source of so much disruption that he was dismissed within a few months.

Returning home, he embarked on a life of crime, specializing in thievery and drug peddling. After a jail sentence of a few months he was paroled, and since all who met him recognized his intelligence, he was referred for psychiatric treatment as a requirement of his parole.

He had done extensive reading in psychology and during the first session he began an intellectual duel with the therapist. He quoted Sartre, Jung, and Freud. He sought to establish that a hedonistic, amoral life was most natural for man and that society decays because it seeks to restrain such impulses. His was a marvelously reasoned disquisition and this brief description does not do him justice. In any event, his preoccupation with this philosophical issue subsided and he found himself attacking the therapist directly for the hypocrisy involved in asking payment for treatment. He was so rabid in his full-scale attack against what he saw as hypocritical self-righteousness that even he could not fail to see that this attack was really meant for his mother.

With this insight the floodgates opened and his rage against his mother poured out. For months he railed against her insincerity, her self-serving piety, and the pathogenic environment she provided for the nurturing of her children. She was the worst, he felt, simply the worst human being he had ever met. Only long after was he able to see her hypocrisy as her own adaptation to her inner psychic needs, her adaptation to her own early troubled childhood, and finally a synthesis of these solutions in her attempt to deal with her environment, the generally hostile white environment.

He said he had reason to be angry with her, but felt that his anger, even considering *her* character, was excessive. He raised the question whether her dominant role in the family, in particular her role with regard to the father and her sons, might not be the role she sought but the role that was given her. She had, after all, been a retarding, inhibiting influence on all the males while giving a boost to her daughter. Seeing that she came from the South, he thought it may have had survival value for women to keep men bridled.

It seems such a common finding that black men feel hostility toward their mothers that some explanation is in order to spell out the climate in which such a disorder of character structure develops. To do so we must make another excursion into "slavery time."

With a fairly realistic idea of the milieu of the slave, the culture which was forced on him, and the universal tasks associated with child-rearing, we might attempt a retrospective construction of child-rearing among slaves between 1665 and 1865 in the United States. From the beginning of their enslavement, all slaves had been confronted with the option to "submit or die," and obviously those who survived to rear children had chosen to live and therefore to submit.

The attack on their autonomy was relentless. Each day they were given the option to work or die, obey or die, and with each day the role, the identity of slave became more real. To live, for a black man, was to submit completely, holding back no part of himself, but yielding up all vestiges of humanity to the slave owner, or at least giving the appearance of doing so. Surely there were brave men who rebelled against the system, rose up and slew the oppressor, and escaped to the North. But *the mother* who remained saw a hundred tortured and killed for every successful rebel. With reality so harsh, with the odds so much against the defiant, what can we speculate about her rearing of her child?

It is reported that newly captured African women slew their children rather than have them reared as slaves. Their decision was a significant one for us, because the infanticide speaks clearly of her knowledge of the options —*she* must kill her child, for if she lets him live it is *she* who must raise him to be a slave. Once the mother opts for her child's life she assumes the task of conveying to him the nature of the world in which he will live and teaching him how to survive in it. In effect, she had to take the role of slave master, treat the child with capricious cruelty, hurt him physically and emotionally, and demand that he respond in an obsequious helpless manner—a manner she knew would enhance his chances of survival. She had to take particular pains to crush any defiant, aggressive traits. No maturity could be allowed; no independence could be encouraged. He must, in fact, learn to treat himself as chattel, his body and person as valuable only as the owner placed value on them. He must learn to fear and exalt the owner and to hate himself. This last comment might well be repeated: in order to survive as a slave, the child had to learn to abandon the usual narcissistic investment of self; he had to be taught to hate himself.

> The story is told of the old slave seen walking along a rough road barefoot with a new pair of shoes in his hand. When asked why he did not protect his feet by wearing the shoes, he replied that he was saving the shoes—"The feet belong to my master but the shoes belong to me!"

It is inconceivable that a man could love and value himself and survive as a slave.

Early in her handling of the child the mother had to demand complete obedience from him. She dared not allow him to grow up expecting love and loving concern. She had to demand that he always show his parents the greatest respect, whether they seemed to earn it or not. On this pattern would be built the later relationship with the owner, and the less conflict he experienced in connection with obedience, the greater the likelihood of survival.

Child-rearing among slaves was never allowed to get beyond the crucial issue of survival. At all times, all slaves were in danger of their lives, and only their thorough knowledge of slavehood offered them a chance of survival. Whatever else was taught the child, it was taught in the context of survival instructions. Black mothers say as they punish rebellious sons: "I'd rather kill him myself than let those white folks get him. He's got to learn."

He had to learn even in the twentieth century to submit. Child-rearing practices are slow to change. The vigorous psychological trends evoked by slavery, their contradiction and confluence, are impressive even when at this distance in time we attempt a reconstruction.

As the literature shows regarding the reaction of Jews under Nazi persecution, the victims of such horrors often experience bizarre reactions. The institution of slavery will call forth a tendency on the part of the enslaved to identify with the oppressor. It is a desperate trick the victim plays on himself. Feeling his own position to be completely hopeless, he executes a series of mental gymnastics, ceases to feel that he is himself, and begins to perceive himself as the one with power, his oppressor. He takes on the personal characteristics of the oppressor and treats his fellow sufferers with the same cruelty he has himself only recently suffered. This maneuver is a desperate, last-ditch neurotic estrangement from reality. In its milder forms it is seen commonly in contemporary America, but we meet nothing comparable to this outright abandonment of reality.

This phenomenon, however, must have been a regular occurrence among slaves who lived permanently in a hopeless state. It therefore requires little imagination to speculate that the slave mother, in her cruelty to her child, found her hand strengthened by this paradoxical reaction of her own. She must often have projected her own feelings of helplessness onto the child and taken the strength and power of the master for her own. In fact, it might be at that very moment of cruelty that she would feel most helpless and find it necessary to resort to some neurotic flight, however bizarre, from the events at hand.

To whatever extent this is done, it reinforces the experience as a training, a warning of dangers to come for the child. For in that moment the mother has become slaveowner and the child the helpless slave.

The grotesque task imposed on the slave mother seems unendurable, and many a mother who embarked on such a path must have come to a point she could in fact not bear. And turning away meant either infanticide or exposing her child to death at the hands of the owners. Population studies are scanty, but what is available suggests an extremely high infant mortality rate among the slaves.

The endurance of slavery as an institution for such a long time introduces the selective factor of survival. For who would survive and rear children to be slaves and survive—who but those willing to submit? And thus the population began to be replenished by slaves who in some measure were willing to be slaves or to give the appearance of it. One might comment that even those who were newly transported from Africa had chosen to be slaves rather than die.

Thus it was in the time of bondage.

And who would say it is so very different now? Must not the black mother warn her child against travel to certain parts of the nation? Does she not fear that any involvement with the police may result in the forfeiture of his life? And does she not know that there remains a national purpose to keep him poor, ill housed, ill trained, and available for the exploitation of his labor? The differences are quantitative, not qualitative, and the mother now and then takes a long, hard look at her world, and a long look at her son, and makes the decision. While she will give him life, she must wound him deeply so that he can survive and pass on the gift. In so doing she forfeits his love for her. She must hurt him first, then he will live, but there will ever be a hatred for her.

Child-rearing is a delicate process, bound irrevocably to the reality of the society. The grim cycle described above will not change until the society into which the mother brings her child ceases to treat him with such cruelty that he must be inoculated with the same hurt by his own mother.

An antisocial, delinquent character problem which grows out of a neurotic mother, father, and family structure roars off like a forest fire when the soil has been so well prepared as this.

Even years later, after it all turned out well, it is still not clear whether the diagnosis was accurate or in fact whether there is any diagnosis in the "manual" to describe his trouble.

He was bizarre. He wore ragged clothes, sat shielding his face from the therapist, and complained of eerie things, such as not knowing when he was hungry and going days at a time without eating simply because he never thought about it. He said he would lose track of time and sit gazing fixedly out the window for hours.

He had a graduate degree, but in recent years had worked in the post office and gradually let his affairs drift. Now unemployed, he had sold his car and was existing on the small savings he had accumulated. He had been hospitalized, received shock treatment, and spent months in closed wards. But now he drifted like a spring gradually coming unwound.

He felt that his strange personality dated back to his mother's death when he was six. She had been a poorly trained schoolteacher who doted on her two children.

She was given to spinning long tales about slavery and the "old times." She had curious ideas about health and deportment. Wash before meals, guard against germs—but she sewed the children into underwear in the fall and cut them out in spring. They were to sit straight at the dinner table, always say "yes, sir" and "no, ma'am," but she fed them mainly grits, syrup, and biscuits. The patient was devoted to her and her death was as anachronistic as her life had been. One evening she complained of a stomach pain and by morning she was dead. He was told she had "acute indigestion."

The father was a bungler, an ineffective small business-man and a teacher. He was fond of quoting the scripture but found himself accused more than once of theft, assault, and other delinquent acts. The children were left with the idea that the appearance of achievement was more important than the substance. They learned to dress properly, to be circumspect in conduct, and to study long hours. They managed to memorize course material but they seemed unable to relate what they learned to the world in which they lived.

Our patient progressed faster than his younger sister but both obtained degrees. It seemed natural, or at least not unnatural, for the sister to bear a child out of wedlock as a result of a casual relationship. She was on welfare for a while before obtaining a minor clerical position which allowed her to eke out an existence for herself and her children. The patient, after completing his training, which prepared him for several kinds of good jobs, obtained work in the post office, apparently only partly because of racial discrimination. He felt that other jobs were not available to him.

It was his symptoms, though, that have significance for us. He spoke of his stomach as not revealing to him his need for food. He said that his legs kept moving down a hall and he found himself out on the street when he should have gone into an office to inquire about a job. His attention was called to the way he spoke of different parts of his body as if they were not a part of him or not under his control. He said that this was the way his mother spoke to her children. He noticed it, in fact, in the way his sister dealt with her own children. He recalled that it was related to his parents' conception of children. They thought of children as affectionate small beings, with no minds, requiring training and discipline. In fact, their conception of people generally followed a similar pattern. He was struck by the difference in their ideas about the occasional white person who entered the family's orbit. Only there were the parents concerned about the individual's *feelings,* only there was a man's emotional reaction seen as having validity and as being of significance. In retrospect, he was driven to the conclusion that his parents must have incorporated a prevalent attitude in the South —that Negroes were a breed of rather placid, empty, but trainable subhumans.

This percept, together with the other events which contributed to his schizoid character structure, had an important part in fashioning his symptoms. Here was a sick man, fortunately now well, whose sickness could only be understood in terms of history.

## The Black Norm

We submit that it is necessary for a black man in America to develop a profound distrust of his white fellow citizens and of the nation. He must be on guard to protect himself against physical hurt. He must cushion himself against cheating, slander, humiliation, and outright mistreatment by the official representatives of society. If he does not so protect himself, he will live a life of such pain and shock as to find life itself unbearable. For his own survival, then, he must develop a *cultural paranoia* in which every white man is a potential enemy unless proved otherwise and every social system is set against him unless he personally finds out differently.

Every black man in America has suffered such injury as to be realistically sad about the hurt done him. He must, however, live in spite of the hurt and so he learns to know his tormentor exceedingly well. He develops a sadness and intimacy with misery which has become a characteristic of black Americans. It is a *cultural depression* and a *cultural masochism*.

He can never quite respect laws which have no respect for him, and laws designed to protect white men are viewed as white men's laws. To break another man's law may be inconvenient if one is caught and punished, but it can never have the moral consequences involved in breaking one's own law. The result may be described as a *cultural antisocialism,* but it is simply an accurate reading of one's environment—a gift black people have developed to a high degree, to keep alive.

These and related traits are simply adaptive devices developed in response to a peculiar environment. They are no more pathological than the compulsive manner in which a diver checks his equipment before a dive or a pilot his parachute. They represent normal devices for "making it" in America, and clinicians who are interested in the psychological functioning of black people must get acquainted with this body of character traits which we call the *Black Norm*. It is a normal complement of psychological devices, and to find the amount of sickness a black man has, one must first total all that appears to represent illness and then subtract the Black Norm. What remains is illness and a proper subject for therapeutic endeavor. To regard the Black Norm as pathological and attempt to remove such traits by treatment would be akin to analyzing away a hunter's cunning or a banker's prudence. This is a body of characteristics essential to life for black men in America and woe be unto that therapist who does not recognize it.

## A Word on the Nature of Mental Illness and Treatment

Mental illness arises from a conflict between the inner drives pushing for individual gratification and the group demands of the external environment. The method of expressing inner needs has developed in contact with and in response to the environment provided by the parents and that segment of the broader society which impinges on the child. It is as if the child takes into himself a part of the world he experiences while quite young and makes that an integral part of his inner self. It is the synthesis of his own personal drives and his early, now incorporated, environment that he subsequently elaborates into his inner self and it is this which is in conflict with the external world.

Something must change—his inner world, the outer world, or both. Too much psychotherapy involves striving only for a change in the inner world and a consequent adaptation to the world outside. Black people cannot abide this and thoughtful therapists know it. A black man's soul can live only if it is oriented toward a change of the social order. A good therapist helps a man change his inner life so that he can more effectively change his outer world.

Finally, psychotherapy itself is an indifferent instrument, profoundly effective in the hands of an artist, and worse than a waste of time in the hands of an incompetent. The interpretations and constructions are important, but a lot of patients have been made well with inexact interpretations. The essential ingredient is the capacity of the therapist to love his patient—to say to him that here is a second chance to organize his inner life, to say that you have a listener and companion who wants you to make it. If you must weep, I'll wipe your tears. If you must hit someone, hit me, I can take it. I will, in fact, do *anything* to help you be what you can be—my love for you is of such an order.

How many people, black or white, can so open their arms to a suffering black man?

Contempt and hatred of black people is so thoroughly a part of the American personality that a profound convulsion of society may be required to help a dark child over his fear of the dark.

# ⟪ IX ⟫

# How Come There's So Much Hate?

When the man died, his wife of forty years was pitied by her friends. The widow was a stern New Englander; her dead husband was a black. In spite of strong social disapproval of their marriage, they had raised children and prospered. There had been some discord between them, but they handled it discreetly and the children had never heard them comment on racial matters. Even when a racial incident was prominent in the news, not a word was said about it. The children assumed that their mother had long since accepted the realities of marriage to a black man. They were completely unprepared for her words when her husband died: "Thank God that nigger is gone!"

Until very recently, psychoanalytic papers dealing with Negroes were very few indeed. In fact, not long ago a study of the literature revealed that more scholarly works had been devoted to the psychological functioning of American Indians than to the psyche of Negroes. Articles dealing primarily with anti-Negro prejudice were even fewer. There have been, nevertheless, a sufficient number of passing references to the subject—as well as the voluminous material on anti-Semitism—to extract a clear summary of the psychoanalytic explanations of anti-Negro feelings. These studies suggest essentially that the unconscious basis for anti-Negro racial prejudice rests on the representation of the black man as an important figure in the unconscious who is both loved or feared and hated. By displacing primarily hateful attitudes onto black people, a person can act upon these feelings, since love and fear are withheld from such displacement.

In this manner black people may represent parents, children, brothers, strangers, the self, or indeed any person about whom contrary feelings are held. Moreover, black skin and alienness make such a psychological maneuver more inviting, for these attributes remove him even further from the real object of the hostile feelings.

At another level the black man is the recipient of projected feelings which are unacceptable, and when such base attitudes are lodged with him, he is then punished for harboring them.

If this description of the theoretical explanation of racial prejudice seems too sketchy, we invite the reader to examine the literature himself. The number of studies is increasing, but the fundamental ideas offered to explain the phenomenon remain few. Many of the studies provide excellent discussions of intrapsychic operations, but in our opinion we have not yet been given an adequate explanation for the intensity of ambivalence that could keep anti-Negro animosity alive after forty years of marriage.

Even more pressing is the question: How is it that so many Mississippians, for example, exhibit intense hatred of black people whereas relatively few Canadians do so? Individuals in both groups experience more or less the same vicissitudes in the course of growing up. Blacks are seen often enough by Canadians. And if it is suggested that the greater number of black people in Mississippi engenders the stronger hostility there, then there are classic studies which seem to show that close association with the object of prejudice tends to minimize hostile feelings.

We must say that the explanations are disappointingly vague and even ambiguous for so sharp and intense a phenomenon. How can there be ambiguity when a widow's epitaph for her mate of forty years is: "Thank God that nigger is gone!"

A young white man sought treatment after his wife had left him. He was depressed and obsessively recounted the details of his brief marriage. Finally he telephoned his wife and pleaded with her to return. She was contemptuous, and he shouted: "Goddammit, treat me like a white man!"

There were, no doubt, a number of factors which brought this phrase to his lips, but it is a common enough phrase, available to anyone, expressing as it does a certain set of attitudes about how blacks and whites are to be treated.

We must distinguish between individual psychological reasons for the development of anti-black feelings and a pervasive climate of prejudice which stimulates and evokes the potential of race prejudice in everyone.

It has been said that studying individual psychological reasons for racial prejudice without examining the culture in which it thrives is like studying the microscopic structure of a kernel of corn to explain its yield without taking account of the climate of sunshine and rainfall in which it will grow.

We suggest that in Mississippi the faintest suggestion of racial prejudice in an individual will be stimulated by that climate to an overgrowth of hatred of blacks. White Southerners themselves seem often the most pitiful victims of this culturally imposed attitude. One is amazed to find brilliant, cultured men of the world whose hatred of blacks reaches pathological proportions. They give the impression of being reasonable, balanced men in all ways except this. And here it is as if an attitude actually foreign to their general nature has been forced on them.

The Southerner may be a different kind of victim.

A white journalist wrote of the last days of his grandfather. The old man had owned a large plantation, which was parceled out to numerous black sharecroppers. He felt that he had a good relationship with them and that he understood them. Through the years he had told his grandson how happy and contented the blacks were. But as the old man began to fail, he underwent mild aberrations. Then, during his last days, he began to suffer delusions that black men were coming after him. Men whom he had patronized and had convinced himself were happy were now turning on him. Small children whom he felt were passive were now, in his delusional state, angry, furious, and eager to tear him limb from limb.

Word-of-mouth reports from the South suggest that such deathbed delusions are not uncommon.

The intensity of anti-black feelings among Southerners is such that it cuts across all religious, moral, national, and economic bounds. Even bonds of kinship give way before the hatred. It is a unique state of affairs when millions of people will conspire and collude to conceal the murderer of a black child. It is monstrous that not one voice was heard to say "This is the man!" when scores of people knew who murdered those black children in a church in Birmingham, Alabama.

Of all the people who have come to the South from all over the world, representing every variation of thought and philosophy, how many have stood up and said: "This is perfidious!"

How many religious men have stated from the pulpit that their congregation's behavior is a stench in the nostrils of God?

How many philosophers and educators have publicly declared that their southern neighbors forfeit their claim on humanity by their bestial acts?

Of all the millions of Southerners, brave and cowardly alike, men who have decried the oppression of blacks have been almost nonexistent.

Further, we are not among those who would dismiss all white Southerners as innately evil men. Rather, we consider them essentially no different from most Americans. Both their kindness and their hatred reach limits not approached in most of their countrymen, but they are essentially mild exaggerations of tendencies common to most Americans. They are closer to the agrarian way of life, but the nation generally considers itself a people descended from farmers. They are simply Americans of the southern variant—with one exception: they live in that area of the nation which was condemned for slaveholding and which by its refusal to relinquish its slaves had them forcibly taken away. While it is a clear historical fact that the pertinent *reasons* behind the Civil War did not include freeing the slaves, still this was the emotional issue offered the public and upon which it waged the war. Out of the conflict there settled over the South the distillate of the viciousness of slavery. Slaves had been held in most states of the Union, but the horror of the system seemed to be connected only with the South.

The quality of cruelty expressed toward blacks became a part of the regional character, imposed on the South by the nation at large. In a sense the United States had cleansed itself of the guilt of slavery at the expense of the principal but by no means exclusive offenders.

We do not suggest that the adoption or acceptance of this role was entirely passive, for one can easily imagine the embittered losers turning with vengeance on the blacks. Ex-slaveowners may in fact have welcomed the role of the cruel oppressor, but we only suggest that, whether it was welcome or not, they had no choice.

And it is this climate of bigotry, remaining largely unchanged to this day, which surrounds Southerners and shapes their attitudes toward blacks. The regional character of the South includes as a dominant theme a contempt and hatred for blacks which reaches irrational extremes.

The atrocities committed by Southerners against blacks are carried out by a few, but with the silent assent of the majority. There is no outrage, no revulsion, no call to conscience; rather, there is a tacit agreement that such things happen because of a "few hotheads"—who are criticized but are nevertheless protected by the social body. There is agreement that "people feel strongly about such things down here" and "we don't want outsiders butting in."

It is a region with an exaggeration of character—but no more than an exaggeration, for Southerners share the American character and their attitudes are shared to a lesser degree by all Americans.

A potentiality for race hatred will be stimulated in any American by the influence of the national or regional character. Southerners will become virulent in their hatred of blacks, others less so, but all will hate and fear the ex-bondsmen.

Under these skies, then, the individual intrapsychic development of racial prejudice unfolds in the form described by psychoanalytic theoreticians. The dynamics of this individual phenomenon operate in an understandable fashion, but they have been set in motion and stimulated to growth by the social climate.

In 1964, California citizens were allowed to vote on a proposition which in effect would have repealed an existing "fair housing" law.

The issue was widely publicized, the proposal was heavily financed, and it was voted into law.

During the campaign a wealthy white woman produced a series of rationalizations explaining why she was voting for the proposition. Although she lived in a large area of expensive homes and although her own home cost $150,-000, she said she was most afraid of black people taking over her neighborhood.

The outrageously irrational quality of racial prejudice is evident in many aspects of the phenomenon. Housing bias is an example of a more far-reaching and influential effect. White people have a deep and abiding feeling that the races are supposed to be separated and that the preferential places should be reserved for themselves.

To live near blacks or to eat with blacks is to jeopardize one's status. White people are supposed to eat and live in better places than black people.

The following example may help to illustrate how central is the attitude of white superiority in this country.

The value of a home has come to be determined neither by the quality of the structure nor by the value of the structures around it. It can be sharply devalued by the proximity of a family of blacks. It is devalued because few other white families would purchase it, and unless it is sought by other black families, the owner finds its market value very low indeed.

We know of no other ethnic group which by its mere proximity can so certainly make a man's home repugnant to him.

The wealthy woman in the example above was so troubled by the prospect of blacks moving into her neighborhood that she took a passionate stand for restrictive legislation in the hope of barring them more effectively. She seemed completely unaware that the number of black people in the market for $150,000 homes is very,

very small and surely presents no threat to her affluent neighborhood.

Such attitudes suggest not only that proximity to blacks lowers a white person's status but that some of the low status of blacks "rubs off" on whites.

In the area of sexual congress between races, prejudice reaches truly heroic heights of idiocy.

The culture seems to require that white people react with horror and revulsion to the idea of the sexual act occurring between whites and blacks. But the following incident is not unusual.

A white girl told her mother that she had become engaged to a Negro. The mother fainted.

On recovering, she asked: "What color is he?" Next she asked: "Does he have money?" And finally: "What does he do?"

Her questions indicate that she was so shocked by her daughter's engagement to a black that she had to search for some way to avoid its being known (if he were fair) or some way for it not to matter (if he were very rich) or some way to neutralize the effect partially (if he had a powerful position).

She sounds very knowledgeable about the culture. She knows that, although everyone will react with shock to the news, people will really care less if the man is not a readily recognizable black. And even that will matter less if he is rich enough or powerful enough.

A few years ago a southern mayor, who all his public life had hewed to the line of white superiority, was swindled by a black man on the streets of a northern city as the mayor tried to contact a black prostitute.

The culture seems to require that white people find sexual contact with blacks too horrible to contemplate—and white people comply with that requirement in their public behavior.

Their private attitudes are another matter. They find black people attractive sexually and subscribe to the almost universal myth of their sexual superiority.

Here again the impress of the culture is important in determining the quality and quantity of the individual response. The culture designates Negroes as sexually superior and uninhibited in their behavior. It further requires that whites view them with contempt and sexual congress with them with horror.

The effect is a weak rather than a strong barrier, since the same culture has defined all sexual acts as debased and forbidden. To describe intercourse with blacks in the same but only stronger terms imposes little restraint. As a result, sexual contact between the races is barred primarily by a superficial public disapproval.

But behind the curtain of public disapproval there remains the intense sexual interest in exotic partners and the individual psychological reaction to a person of a different color and a different class. Public opposition has thus served to heighten the sexual interest black people have for whites.

It seems inaccurate to apply the term "racial prejudice" both to Negroes' feelings about white people and to their feelings about themselves. There seems to be confusion about the quality of one's feelings if one is a victim of racial prejudice. The fact of the matter is that black people are inclined to regard the white man as superior. There are examples without number in the patois and the everyday behavior of millions of blacks which speak for the fact that they do indeed feel that the white man is intrinsically better.

Caution must be exercised in distinguishing feelings of inferiority from emulation of the majority by a minority concerned with survival. But, even taking this into account, there remains an increment of feeling which says emphatically: "White is right."

> For a black man to straighten his hair chemically, to have what is known as a "process," is a painful, dangerous procedure. The result is a slick pompadour which in no way save one resembles a white man's hair. Only in that it is straight and not kinky does it appear less black and more white.

> Negroes have always referred to straight hair as good— and kinky hair as bad.

Black people feel that white people are smarter, and here there is a subtle refinement. It is not that they see themselves in a real sense personally as stupid. It is rather that they look upon themselves as average and the white man as "super-smart." Black racists are fond of recounting the evil genius of the American white man, and a careful hearing of their words tells clearly that, though they *say* that they no longer look up to Charlie, this is by no means the case. They have simply reversed the moral value placed on his acts. Now they are evil and perfidious, whereas before they were glorious and enviable. But they continue to be brilliant acts of genius, executed by omniscient men. It is a pity that too many of these voices calling Negroes to blackness still preach a thinly veiled version of white supremacy.

Consider too what would be proper conduct if one were an oppressed member of a helpless minority held in effective bondage by a majority which not only has numbers in its favor but is a majority of intellectual supermen as well. If a person had such a view, he would develop an extremely suspicious way of life. He would adopt a frightened, cornered, panicky, paranoid way of thinking.

We suspect that many of the black racists exhibit a paranoid style of life because they feel they are facing an enemy of supermen, not simply an enemy which outnumbers them.

Such an attitude need not be confined to racists.

A black professional was conversing with a younger man about a new project. He answered several questions about the proposal, some parts of which involved confrontation with white professionals. The older man was held in high esteem by black people in the community. He had a distinguished record of service on community-wide committees and boards. To an outsider, he was as comfortable at a mixed cocktail party as in his office. His professional activities were wide and multiracial. By almost any measure he would be regarded as successful.

As the exchange continued, to each question the older man raised an objection. He warned against angering "them." "They" might not like it; "they" would have thought of it first; "they" would have a different and therefore better proposal. He got angrier as the discussion continued. "They" became increasingly synonymous with all white people.

He finally became exasperated and ended the conversation with "Don't you know Charlie never sleeps?"

It must be apparent how profoundly damaging such an attitude can be to the achievement of black people. In the United States at this time the essential competition between men is an intellectual one. The essential judgment of one's usefulness rests on one's intellectual capability, and if one fails in *fair* competition, it is an intellectual failure. Second only to making certain that black people have a fair chance is the necessity that they be free of corrosive attitudes about their intellectual inferiority.

In the area of ambition and striving there is a further consequence of this attitude. The conviction that Charlie is shrewder saps a black man's drive. It is a discouraging task to compete against a superman even if he is "super" only in one's own mind. Humans being what they are, it provides an opportunity to opt out of the struggle altogether and develops an attitude of "What's the use? Why fight it? You can't possibly win struggling as ordinary men struggle; ordinary men sleep nights and Charlie never sleeps."

The only way out, if indeed it can be so considered, is a poor one at best and the price paid for success is terribly high. We speak of those Negroes who make it by emulating the white man. They accept as a fact that Negroes are not so smart as white people and decide to reject their blackness and, insofar as possible, embrace whiteness. They identify with white men in every way and add to that a contempt for black people. In the process they gain some of the "white man's magic." They acquire some of the superior qualities they attribute to him. They may as a result feel more competent, but it is a direct function of their feeling that "other Negroes" are incompetent. In this way they develop a contempt for themselves, because, however much they avoid it, they remain black, and there are things about themselves that will yet remind them of their blackness and those reminders will evoke feelings of self-hatred and self-depreciation.

To the extent that emulation of the white man is rewarded by society, the individual will find confirmation of his belief that this is the proper course. If he achieves status and wealth, these gains may well be saying to him that "white is right." His psychic division widens and his hatred of self grows. The more success he gains, the more he feels white people are in fact smarter, and the more convinced he is that black people are stupid.

For any person growing up in the often anti-intellectual climate of America, it is difficult, whether he be black or white, to develop an accurate assessment of and a healthy respect for his own intellectual endowment. Imagine how difficult this is when every element in the milieu says that your kind is stupid and their kind is smart. A society which can deal out such severe punishment and which can offer such magnificent rewards is most persuasive, however foolish its message may be.

Black men hear on all sides that success lies in being like white people, who establish the standard of wisdom. Is it any wonder, then, that this consequence of racial prejudice is deadly to the intellectual flowering of black people? And is it any wonder, then, that in a desperate attempt to avoid it, many latter-day chauvinists adopt an anti-intellectual posture? They fail to see that by this very stance they reveal themselves as victims of the same American creed of white superiority.

A black domestic stated that she never worked for Negroes because she found them to be more demanding, more critical, and less willing to pay. She said that her white employers were more generous with gifts, more willing to overlook occasional loafing on the job, and rarely suspicious of her stealing.

Without doubt, her observations are accurate. The black employer can more easily identify with the black employee and can readily imagine being exploited by the employee. A black person has heard so many tales of a clever servant outwitting the master that he is alert to being so taken in.

He may experience such an intense identification with the white man that he may be determined to be an even more hard-driving master than those he has heard about. The more harshly he treats the black man beneath him, the further he lifts himself into the white world. Or at least so it may seem. In fact, however, he builds for himself an ever more deadly snare and those occasions when he is acutely reminded of his blackness become more and more painful. Inasmuch as he is black, he must, by the inexorable laws that govern us, feel toward himself exactly as he feels toward his servant.

But though the employer is guilty, so also is the

servant. He feels that his employer, being black, is not so grand as his white counterpart and therefore he gains less in reflected glory. He thinks that all blacks are brothers and that his employer is "no better than me." He cannot then establish the same relationship as with a white employer, who he feels is better than he.

Moreover, both employer and servant live in a country which has as one of its fundamental tenets that all black men are equally base. They can then only feel that any relationship which sets one over the other is a sham and a pretense and ought to be done away with.

It is a relationship most revealing about black prejudice against blacks.

Religion plays a role in the cancer of black self-depreciation and the exaltation of whites. All religions urge their adherents to look beyond the problems of the day to some major guiding principle or to the will of some superior being or to follow certain rules that will assure happiness in an after life. Religion teaches that one should in general be kind, be fair, be modest, restrain impulses, and love everyone.

It is designed to evoke guilt, and in that regard it begins with the assumption that mortals are inherently wicked and can gain pardon and find a welcome into the house of God only by some extraordinary act of faith.

An initial assumption of guilt, if taken seriously, may or may not cripple white Americans, but it is lethal to black men. They have grown up in an environment which has labeled them wicked and base. If, in trying to find solace from the horrors of their lives, they turn to a religion or in fact a deity who requires that they admit wickedness before comfort is given, they may find it difficult to distinguish the white man's view of them as wicked from the church's view of them as wicked.

The unfortunate result is generally an acceptance by black people of their sinfulness in order to feel some relief from guilt. The sinfulness they admit to and forswear is sinfulness and evil as defined by white America in regard to black men.

Sins become wrongdoings, in terms established by white men, who have every reason to want to pacify black people. Stealing, fighting, gambling, licentious and irresponsible acts become matters of supreme importance and the full weight of religious orthodoxy is turned against them.

Since these are acts of which society says black men for the most part are guilty, by these definitions few white men are burdened by "sins." (Large-scale dishonesty and the abuse of power are rarely defined as sinful.) The religious structure has thus reinforced the view that white men are superior and black men inferior.

As discussed here, Christianity is the greatest offender, but any religion which elevates guilt-stimulating attitudes about sin and debasement to the level of the supernatural would echo this nation's attitudes toward Negroes for any black man who in that religion sought comfort.

Negroes are black before they are religionists and are encouraged by national attitudes to develop disgust and contempt for bad, black, "nigger-like" behavior. We submit that when at a later date they are encouraged to reject sin, they see the two as identical and turn away from the same sets of debased acts. The result is the pious, white, freshly laundered Negro, sans dirt, sans sin, and sans soul.

The idea of integration likewise contains the same cultural element, carrying the implication that it is better to mingle with whites and be accepted into their company than to be excluded. But again it is the white man who determines which black man will be worthy of his company, since no black man can integrate any situation. White people must invite black people in or, more accurately, must lower the barriers and *allow* them entry. Those so blessed gain grace through proximity to whites and, by this selective process and the advantages which flow from it, is the cultural attitude of white supremacy and black inferiority maintained.

While the contemporary concept of "blackness" is a mixed blessing, surely one of its chief virtues has been the removal from white hands of the power to anoint any black man by allowing him to integrate and to reap some substantive benefits. By denouncing integration as a senseless, irrelevant, and unpraiseworthy goal, blacks at least weakened what had come to be a social perversion.

For black and white alike, the air of this nation is perfused with the idea of white supremacy and everyone grows to manhood under this influence. Americans find that it is a basic part of their nationhood to despise blacks. No man who breathes this air can avoid it and black men are no exception. They are taught to hate themselves, and if at some point they discover that they are the object of this hatred, they are faced with an additional task, nothing less, for the imperative remains—Negroes are to be despised.

Thus the dynamics of black self-hatred are unique.

They involve the child's awareness that all people who are black as he is are so treated by white people. Whatever hostility he mounts against white people finds little support in the weakness and the minority status of black people. As it is hopeless for him to consider righting this wrong by force, he identifies with his oppressor psychologically in an attempt to escape from his hopeless position. From his new psychologically "white" position, he turns on black people with aggression and hostility and hates blacks and, among the blacks, himself.

Racial prejudice, therefore, is a pitiful product of systematized cruelty, in which frightened people climb onto the stand with the oppressor and say: "Yes, we hate them too!" They are opportunists, wretched and terrified, but going with a winner.

# ⟨ X ⟩

# *Black Rage*

History may well show that of all the men who lived during our fateful century none illustrated the breadth or the grand potential of man so magnificently as did Malcolm X. If, in future chronicles, America is regarded as the major nation of our day, and the rise of darker people from bondage as the major event, then no figure has appeared thus far who captures the spirit of our times as does Malcolm.

Malcolm is an authentic hero, indeed the only universal black hero. In his unrelenting opposition to the viciousness in America, he fired the imagination of black men all over the world.

If this black nobleman is a hero to black people in the United States and if his life reflects their aspirations, there can be no doubt of the universality of black rage.

Malcolm responded to his position in his world and to

his blackness in the manner of so many black boys. He turned to crime. He was saved by a religious sect given to a strange, unhistorical explanation of the origin of black people and even stranger solutions to their problems. He rose to power in that group and outgrew it.

Feeding on his own strength, growing in response to his own commands, limited by no creed, he became a citizen of the world and an advocate of all oppressed people no matter their color or belief. Anticipating his death by an assassin, he distilled, in a book, the essence of his genius, his life. His autobiography thus is a legacy and, together with his speeches, illustrates the thrusting growth of the man—his evolution, rapid, propulsive, toward the man he might have been had he lived.

The essence of Malcolm X was growth, change, and a seeking after truth.

Alarmed white people saw him first as an eccentric and later as a dangerous radical—a revolutionary without troops who threatened to stir black people to riot and civil disobedience. Publicly, they treated him as a joke; privately, they were afraid of him.

After his death he was recognized by black people as the "black shining prince" and recordings of his speeches became treasured things. His autobiography was studied, his life marveled at. Out of this belated admiration came the philosophical basis for black activism and indeed the thrust of Black Power itself, away from integration and civil rights and into the "black bag."

Unlike Malcolm, however, the philosophical underpinnings of the new black militancy were static. They remained encased within the ideas of revolution and black nationhood, ideas Malcolm had outgrown by the time of his death. His stature has made even his earliest statements gospel and men now find themselves willing to die for words which in retrospect are only milestones in the growth of a fantastic man.

Many black men who today preach blackness seem headed blindly toward self-destruction, uncritical of anything "black" and damning the white man for diabolical wickedness. For a philosophical base they have turned to the words of Malcolm's youth.

This perversion of Malcolm's intellectual position will not, we submit, be held against him by history.

Malcolm's meaning for us lies in his fearless demand for truth and his evolution from a petty criminal to an international statesman—accomplished by a black man against odds of terrible magnitude—in America. His message was his life, not his words, and Malcolm knew it.

Black Power activism—thrust by default temporarily at the head of a powerful movement—is a conception that contributes in a significant way to the strength and unity of that movement but is unable to provide the mature vision for the mighty works ahead. It will pass and leave black people in this country prouder, stronger, more determined, but in need of grander princes with clearer vision.

We believe that the black masses will rise with a simple and eloquent demand to which new leaders must give tongue. They will say to America simply:

## "GET OFF OUR BACKS!"

The problem will be so simply defined.
What is the problem?

*The white man has crushed all but the life from blacks from the time they came to these shores to this very day.*

What is the solution?

*Get off their backs.*

How?

*By simply doing it—now.*

This is no oversimplification. Greater changes than this in the relations of peoples have taken place before. The nation would benefit tremendously. Such a change might bring about a closer examination of our relations with foreign countries, a reconsideration of economic policies, and a re-examination if not a redefinition of nationhood. It might in fact be the only change which can prevent a degenerative decline from a powerful nation to a feeble, third-class, ex-colonialist country existing at the indulgence of stronger powers.

In spite of the profound shifts in power throughout the world in the past thirty years, the United States seems to have a domestic objective of "business as usual," with no change needed or in fact wanted.

All the nasty problems are overseas. At home the search is for bigger profits and smaller costs, better education and lower taxes, more vacation and less work, more for me and less for you. Problems at home are to be talked away, reasoned into nonexistence, and put to one side while we continue the great American game of greed.

There is, however, an inevitability built into the natural order of things. Cause and effect are in fact joined, and if you build a sufficient cause then not all the talk or all the tears in God's creation can prevent the effect from presenting itself one morning as the now ripened fruit of your labors.

America began building a cause when black men were first sold into bondage. When the first black mother killed her newborn rather than have him grow into a slave. When the first black man slew himself rather than submit to an organized system of man's feeding upon another's flesh. America had well begun a cause when all the rebels were either slain or broken and the nation set to the task of refining the system of slavery so that the maximum labor might be extracted from it.

The system achieved such refinement that the capital loss involved when a slave woman aborted could be set against the gain to be expected from forcing her into brutish labor while she was with child.

America began building a potent cause in its infancy as a nation.

It developed a way of life, an American ethos, a national life style which included the assumption that blacks are inferior and were born to hew wood and draw water. Newcomers to this land (if white) were immediately made to feel welcome and, among the bounty available, were given blacks to feel superior to. They were required to despise and depreciate them, abuse and exploit them, and one can only imagine how munificent this land must have seemed to the European—a land with built-in scapegoats.

The hatred of blacks has been so deeply bound up with being an American that it has been one of the first things new Americans learn and one of the last things old Americans forget. Such feelings have been elevated to a position of national character, so that individuals now no longer feel personal guilt or responsibility for the oppression of black people. The nation has incorporated this oppression into itself in the form of folkways and storied traditions, leaving the individual free to shrug his shoulders and say only: "That's our way of life."

This way of life is a heavy debt indeed, and one trembles for the debtor when payment comes due.

America has waxed rich and powerful in large measure on the backs of black laborers. It has become a violent, pitiless nation, hard and calculating, whose moments of generosity are only brief intervals in a ferocious narrative of life, bearing a ferocity and an aggression so strange in this tiny world where men die if they do not live together.

With the passing of the need for black laborers, black people have become useless; they are a drug on the market. There are not enough menial jobs. They live in a nation which has evolved a work force of skilled and semi-skilled workmen. A nation which chooses simultaneously to exclude all black men from this favored labor force and to deny them the one thing America has offered every other group—unlimited growth with a ceiling set only by one's native gifts.

The facts, however obfuscated, are simple. Since the demise of slavery black people have been expendable in a cruel and impatient land. The damage done to black people has been beyond reckoning. Only now are we beginning to sense the bridle placed on black children by a nation which does not want them to grow into mature human beings.

The most idealistic social reformer of our time, Martin Luther King, was not slain by one man; his murder grew out of that large body of violent bigotry America has always nurtured—that body of thinking which screams for the blood of the radical, or the conservative, or the villain, or the saint. To the extent that he stood in the way of bigotry, his life was in jeopardy, his saintly persuasion notwithstanding. To the extent that he was black and was calling America to account, his days were numbered by the nation he sought to save.

Men and women, even children, have been slain for no other earthly reason than their blackness. Property and goods have been stolen and the victims then harried and punished for their poverty. But such viciousness can at least be measured or counted.

Black men, however, have been so hurt in their manhood that they are now unsure and uneasy as they teach their sons to be men. Women have been so humiliated and used that they may regard womanhood as a curse and flee from it. Such pain, so deep, and such real jeopardy, that the fundamental protective function of the family has been denied. These injuries we have no way to measure.

Black men have stood so long in such peculiar jeopardy in America that a *black norm* has developed—a suspiciousness of one's environment which is necessary for survival. Black people, to a degree that approaches paranoia, must be ever alert to danger from their white fellow citizens. It is a cultural phenomenon peculiar to black Americans. And it is a posture so close to paranoid thinking that the mental disorder into which black people most frequently fall is paranoid psychosis.

Can we say that white men have driven black men mad?

An educated black woman had worked in an integrated setting for fifteen years. Compliant and deferential, she had earned promotions and pay increases by hard work and excellence. At no time had she been involved in black activism, and her only participation in the movement had been a yearly contribution to the N.A.A.C.P.

During a lull in the racial turmoil she sought psychiatric treatment. She explained that she had lately become alarmed at waves of rage that swept over her as she talked to white people or at times even as she looked at them. In view of her past history of compliance and passivity, she felt that something was wrong with her. If her controls slipped she might embarrass herself or lose her job.

A black man, a professional, had been a "nice guy" all his life. He was a hard-working non-militant who avoided discussions of race with his white colleagues. He smiled if their comments were harsh and remained unresponsive to racist statements. Lately he has experienced almost uncontrollable anger toward his white co-workers, and although he still manages to keep his feelings to himself, he confides that blacks and whites have been lying to each other. There is hatred and violence between them and he feels trapped. He too fears for himself if his controls should slip.

If these educated recipients of the white man's bounty find it hard to control their rage, what of their less fortunate kinsman who has less to protect, less to lose, and more scars to show for his journey in this land?

The tone of the preceding chapters has been mournful, painful, desolate, as we have described the psychological consequences of white oppression of blacks. The centuries of senseless cruelty and the permeation of the black man's character with the conviction of his own hatefulness and inferiority tell a sorry tale.

This dismal tone has been deliberate. It has been an attempt to evoke a certain quality of depression and hopelessness in the reader and to stir these feelings. These are the most common feelings tasted by black people in America.

The horror carries the endorsement of centuries and the entire lifespan of a nation. It is a way of life which reaches back to the beginnings of recorded time. And all the bestiality, wherever it occurs and however long it has been happening, is narrowed, focused, and refined to shine into a black child's eyes when first he views his world. All that has ever happened to black men and women he sees in the victims closest to him, his parents.

A life is an eternity and throughout all that eternity a black child has breathed the foul air of cruelty. He has grown up to find that his spirit was crushed before he knew there was need of it. His ambitions, even in their forming, showed him to have set his hand against his own. This is the desolation of black life in America.

Depression and grief are hatred turned on the self. It is instructive to pursue the relevance of this truth to the condition of black Americans.

Black people have shown a genius for surviving under the most deadly circumstances. They have survived because of their close attention to reality. A black dreamer would have a short life in Mississippi. They are of necessity bound to reality, chained to the facts of the times; historically the penalty for misjudging a situation involving white men has been death. The preoccupation with religion has been a willing adoption of fantasy to prod an otherwise reluctant mind to face another day.

We will even play tricks on ourselves if it helps us stay alive.

The psychological devices used to survive are reminiscent of the years of slavery, and it is no coincidence. The same devices are used because black men face the same danger now as then.

The grief and depression caused by the condition of black men in America is an unpopular reality to the sufferers. They would rather see themselves in a more heroic posture and chide a disconsolate brother. They would like to point to their achievements (which in fact have been staggering); they would rather point to virtue (which has been shown in magnificent form by some blacks); they would point to bravery, fidelity, prudence, brilliance, creativity, all of which dark men have shown in abundance. But the overriding experience of the black American has been grief and sorrow and no man can change that fact.

His grief has been realistic and appropriate. What people have so earned a period of mourning?

We want to emphasize yet again the depth of the grief for slain sons and ravished daughters, how deep and lingering it is.

If the depth of this sorrow is felt, we can then consider what can be made of this emotion.

As grief lifts and the sufferer moves toward health, the hatred he had turned on himself is redirected toward his tormentors, and the fury of his attack on the one who caused him pain is in direct proportion to the depth of his grief. When the mourner lashes out in anger, it is a relief to those who love him, for they know he has now returned to health.

Observe that the amount of rage the oppressed turns on his tormentor is a direct function of the depth of his grief, and consider the intensity of black men's grief.

Slip for a moment into the soul of a black girl whose womanhood is blighted, not because she is ugly, but because she is black and by definition all blacks are ugly.

Become for a moment a black citizen of Birmingham, Alabama, and try to understand his grief and dismay when innocent children are slain while they worship, for no other reason than that they are black.

Imagine how an impoverished mother feels as she watches the light of creativity snuffed out in her children by schools which dull the mind and environs which rot the soul.

For a moment make yourself the black father whose son went innocently to war and there was slain—for whom, for what?

For a moment be any black person, anywhere, and you will feel the waves of hopelessness that engulfed black men and women when Martin Luther King was murdered. All black people understood the tide of anarchy that followed his death.

It is the transformation of *this* quantum of grief into aggression of which we now speak. As a sapling bent low stores energy for a violent backswing, blacks bent double by oppression have stored energy which will be released in the form of rage—black rage, apocalyptic and final.

White Americans have developed a high skill in the art of misunderstanding black people. It must have seemed to slaveholders that slavery would last through all eternity, for surely their misunderstanding of black bondsmen suggested it. If the slaves were eventually to be released from bondage, what could be the purpose of creating the fiction of their subhumanity?

It must have seemed to white men during the period 1865 to 1945 that black men would always be a passive, compliant lot. If not, why would they have stoked the flames of hatred with such deliberately barbarous treatment?

White Americans today deal with "racial incidents" from summer to summer as if such minor turbulence will always remain minor and one need only keep the blacks busy till fall to have made it through another troubled season.

Today it is the young men who are fighting the battles, and, for now, their elders, though they have given their approval, have not joined in. The time seems near, however, for the full range of the black masses to put down the broom and buckle on the sword. And it grows nearer day by day. Now we see skirmishes, sputtering erratically, evidence if you will that the young men are in a warlike mood. But evidence as well that the elders are watching closely and may soon join the battle.

Even these minor flurries have alarmed the country and have resulted in a spate of generally senseless programs designed to give *temporary summer jobs!!* More interesting in its long-range prospects has been the apparent eagerness to draft black men for military service. If in fact this is a deliberate design to place black men in uniform in order to get them off the street, it may be the most curious "instant cure" for a serious disease this nation has yet attempted. Young black men are learning the most modern techniques for killing—techniques which may be used against *any* enemy.

But it is all speculation. The issue finally rests with the black masses. When the servile men and women stand up, we had all better duck.

We should ask what is likely to galvanize the masses into aggression against the whites.

Will it be some grotesque atrocity against black people which at last causes one-tenth of the nation to rise up in indignation and crush the monstrosity?

Will it be the example of black people outside the United States who have gained dignity through their own liberation movement?

Will it be by the heroic action of a small group of blacks which by its wisdom and courage commands action in a way that cannot be denied?

Or will it be by blacks, finally and in an unpredictable way, simply getting fed up with the bumbling stupid racism of this country? Fired not so much by any one incident as by the gradual accretion of stupidity into fixtures of national policy.

All are possible, or any one, or something yet unthought. It seems certain only that on the course the nation now is headed it will happen.

One might consider the possibility that, if the national direction remains unchanged, such a conflagration simply might *not* come about. Might not black people remain where they are, as they did for a hundred years during slavery?

Such seems truly inconceivable. Not because blacks are so naturally warlike or rebellious, but because they are filled with such grief, such sorrow, such bitterness, and such hatred. It seems now delicately poised, not yet risen to the flash point, but rising rapidly nonetheless. No matter what repressive measures are invoked against the blacks, they will never swallow their rage and go back to blind hopelessness.

If existing oppressions and humiliating disenfranchisements are to be lifted, they will have to be lifted most speedily, or catastrophe will follow.

For there are no more psychological tricks blacks can play upon themselves to make it possible to exist in dreadful circumstances. No more lies can they tell themselves. No more dreams to fix on. No more opiates to dull the pain. No more patience. No more thought. No more reason. Only a welling tide risen out of all those terrible years of grief, now a tidal wave of fury and rage, and all black, black as night.